It's Time To Be Healed

By Delores Winder
With Bill Keith

It's Time To Be Healed

"Books for the Journey"
Stonegate Publishing Co., Inc.
Lubbock 2025

Copyright 2025 © by Bill and Vivian Keith
Stonegate Publishing Co., Inc.
Lubbock, TX 79401
BooksbyStonegate@gmail.com

Selected portions of this publication may be copied within the framework of the Fair Usage Policy.

Also by Bill Keith:

Days of Anguish, Days of Hope
The Commissioner
Whisper in the Wind
The Magic Bullet
Scopes II/the Great Debate
To God Be the Glory
From One Fire
It's All About the Journey
Gettin' Old Ain't for Sissies
Numerous Others

To the Rev. Larry Bass and his dear wife Charlotte who faithfully ministered to the Winders during their final years.

Introduction

Bill and Delores Winder were a happily married couple living in beautiful Portland, Oregon. They were members of the Methodist church where Delores taught a Sunday school class and with Bill ministered to the young people in the church.

But in 1957 their lives were forever changed when Delores was diagnosed with pseudoarthrosis, a disease for which there is no cure.

It's Time to be Healed is her story of the pain and suffering she endured for the next nineteen and one-half years.

But it is also the story of one of the most amazing healing miracles of the 20th Century.

~Bill Keith

Contents

Introduction 1

1. The Shadow of Death 5
2. Days of Anguish 15
3. Strange and Wonderful Ways 25
4. Rise and Be Healed 35
5. Good Times, Bad Times 51
6. The Surrender 73
7. The Ministry 87
8. The Great Physician 101
9. Inner Healing 109
10. Deliverance 125
11. Some Things to Remember 133
12. Walking in Victory 139

Remembrance 149

Commentary: Gifts of the Spirit 153

About the Author 161

The Shadow of Death   1

The doctors said I was dying. I had been sick for 19 ½ years and every minute of it showed on my body. I had stalled the Judgment Day for nearly two decades but my time was running out.

After all the years of sickness and pain I wanted to die. Dying would be easy; enduring more pain unthinkable.

For months death stalked me casting its shadow over my emaciated body.

Some people believe they will live forever but I accepted the fact that my life would soon be over.

During those years life was a living hell. Thank God I was a Christian and knew I was going to heaven. There I finally would be free of the body cast and the neck brace – that were constant burdens – free of hospitals, surgeries, pain, and medications. Free of torment. Free to walk and run again.

"Maybe, God, I'll get the feeling back in my legs! And my arms and body!" I often dreamed out loud. "Oh, it would be so nice to feel my husband's arms around me again and to do something by myself."

Being confined to a body cast and later a wheel chair was difficult for I had always been so fiercely active and independent. After being an invalid all those years, you forget what it's like to be free."

My husband Bill and son Chris were always so very kind and helpful to me.

Our married son Doug, his wife Ann, and our three grandchildren also shared their kindness and love with me.

My doctors called my illness pseudoarthrosis and told me there was no known cure or any way to stop its progression. The only option was to live and die with it.

Here's how they explained the disease. A healthy person's bloodstream contains everything necessary to keep their bones strong. But my bones did not absorb what they needed. Therefore, I developed advanced osteoporosis that caused my bones to become old and brittle.

When the doctors in Portland realized the disease was causing the bones in my back to deteriorate, they hospitalized me from January through April of 1957. During that time, surgeons performed my first spinal fusion, an operation that was intended to hold my crumbling vertebrae in place. They removed a bone for the fusion from the larger of the two bones in one of my legs.

They also ordered a back brace to support my spine and told me I would never be without it again.

But the brace didn't provide enough support and I had to walk bent over to keep my spine from getting caught on the bone spurs that developed at the spinal fusion sites. I had to be very careful to keep these spurs from pulling down more of the vertebrae in my weakened back.

Bill built me a special steel brace. It worked for a

while but had to be worn outside my clothing. The steel supports stuck out at the sides and, as I walked around the house, Bill and Chris would hang dishtowels on the end of my brace. We laughed about it.

Bill joked about feeding me Elmer's Glue to hold me together. He would ask Chris, "How much Elmer's Glue do you think it would take to hold Mama together?"

My dear wonderful Bill who stood faithfully with me during all those years of pain once said, "We have to joke about it to keep from crying."

After my spinal fusion, we had to make quite a lot of adjustments. I couldn't drive our car because the doctor told me that even pushing down on the brake pedal could send my back into shock and break more vertebrae.

But I still could help take care of my family and managed fairly well for two-and-a-half years until the fusion broke.

So, I faced another surgery. The doctors repeated the fusion using a graft from my other leg then placed me in a body caste from under my arms down to my legs.

During the next fifteen years the doctors performed two more fusions.

Since the first three fusions were unsuccessful the doctors decided to perform a frontal fusion in an attempt to bond my crumbling bone to the front of the vertebrae.

This surgery was unbelievable. Once the incision was made, the surgeons removed all the vital organs in the area in order to insert the bone. After fusing the bone, they replaced my organs and closed the incision.

A nurse at the hospital later told me the surgeon ordered her to check me every hour and said he didn't want me lying there dead in a hospital bed.

The frontal fusion held only a short time and then my condition grew rapidly worse and the pain unbearable.

The doctors decided that it would be necessary to perform a percutaneous cordotomy, a procedure usually reserved for terminal patients, but it would control the pain

Prior to the cordotomy the doctors carefully explained the procedure to me. They said the percutaneous cordotomy literally means burning out the nerve centers in the spinal column and that once destroyed the nerve centers could not be restored and the procedure would have permanent consequences.

They also explained that it would involve burning at least six spinal cord segments above the origin of the pain and in order to achieve complete pain relief the entire lateral spinothalamic tract would have to be burned through. If it were not the pain would remain.

Although they tried not to be blunt about it the unmistakable implication was that the cordotomy was being performed only because there was no hope of healing my disease. I was dying and the cordotomy would give me some relief during the final stages of my life.

Using an X-ray to guide them they inserted a needle into my spinal cord and literally burned out the nerve centers completely destroying them.

The cordotomy was a great success because my pain was gone. But there were consequences. I no longer had any feeling from my neck level down on my right side. Hence, I could not lift my feet off the floor. But I was able to walk a little by shuffling my legs along.

During the next year-and-a-half the pain increased so much on the left side of my body that the doctors decided to perform another cordotomy.

Once again, they explained that once the nerve centers from the left side of my body were destroyed the procedure would be irreversible and nerve function could never be restored.

It was also a great success. I no longer felt any pain on the left side of my body where the areas were deadened.

But unfortunately, I still had pain in other parts of my body.

With bilateral cordotomies affecting both of my legs when I tried to walk, I had to carefully watch my feet. My brain had to tell my legs to move since I had no feeling in my feet.

Interestingly, the doctors said they had no idea a person with two cordotomies could shuffle across the floor until they saw me do it.

One surgeon told me, "Delores, you probably will be confined to a wheelchair from now on because we've never known a person with two such procedures that ever walked again."

But the day after the second procedure, I told my doctors, "I want up! I'm going to walk! And I walked in my shuffling fashion."

After all the years of sickness and pain, I began to wonder why I was sick and where my sickness came from. I learned from the Scriptures that it certainly was not caused by God.

When sin came into the world it was accompanied by sickness and disease. Also, Satan himself causes some sicknesses. I believe he put chains of sickness around me and my body had his signature all over it. And when he catches you in a trap, he isn't about to let go.

Although I knew what had happened to me and where my sickness came from, I didn't know what to do about it.

Oh, I knew Jesus but he was in Heaven. And I knew about Satan but I thought he was in hell.

I faithfully read my Bible and believed it to be the infallible Word of God and the truth. Yet because of my church upbringing, I put healing and deliverance back in the days of Jesus and the Apostolic Age and did not believe they were for today.

The only time I heard the term Holy Spirit was when we recited the Apostles' Creed at church and it had been a long time since I had been able to go to church.

Before my illness, Bill and I worked with the young people in our Methodist church. It was frustrating when those kids came to us with problems for which there seemed to be no answers. We just encouraged them to try to be good, attend church, and do their best.

"We'll pray for you," we told them.

But we never said, "We'll pray with you."

"Dear God, there must be more than this to give to these young people," I cried out

Neither did our minister have any answers. While he was visiting me one day, I asked, "What else is there?"

"What do you mean, what else is there?"

"What ever happened to the excitement of being a Christian?"

"Delores, you're always hunting for something you don't have,"

It troubled me that when I read the Bible and saw the New Testament Christians were excited about their faith. But it seemed to me that Bill and I were just going through the motions of being Christians and nothing ever happens.

Day after day, I read the Bible and would think," Wouldn't it have been nice to have lived when Jesus walked here on earth? So many things happened. Were miracles only for the three short years of his ministry and for the ministries of the apostles and disciples who walked with him? I wondered.

I felt as though I was looking at a giant jigsaw puzzle of Christianity with a great big piece missing and no one – not even my minister – could find the missing piece for me.

In the spring of 1975, I went back into the hospital. It had become a constant battle just to keep my body functioning. One of my kidneys closed and the other was constantly infected. My bowels had not moved in several weeks and my stomach troubled me from the time I first entered the body cast fifteen years earlier. Also, my esophagus had ruptured.

My doctors kept me sedated all the time in an attempt to kill the increasing pain but it wasn't working very well. When the pain became unbearable, they gave me stronger painkillers.

I was living on pills to tranquilize me, pills for my ruptured esophagus, pills for my stomach, pills for my kidneys, pills for my heart, pills for my low blood pressure, and pills to help me sleep. My whole world revolved around several little bottles of pills.

I could only eat dry toast, a cup of tea, a small piece of broiled chicken, and instant Chicken Noodle soup from a package. No wonder my invalid body weighed only seventy-three pounds.

Dr. I. I. Van Zandt who had treated me for nine years was a very compassionate man. We became close friends and I called him Van. He had gone through a lot of traumas in his own life and often shared his feelings with me.

I was a good listener. Why not? There wasn't much else for me to do.

The time eventually came when Van and the other doctors lost hope. They knew I was dying and it was just a matter of time.

However, they did call in another neurosurgeon to conduct tests to see if there was anything further that could be done for me. He thoroughly examined me and told Van it was time for me to die,

It was Van's unhappy duty to tell me the results of the final tests the neurosurgeon conducted. He told Van that a person's body can tolerate only so much disease, illness, and pain,

Van really didn't have to tell me the results of the tests. I knew I was dying and looked forward to it.

Van came into my hospital room, walked over to my bed, and said, "Delores, I'm sorry, there's nothing more we can do."

I looked up at the kind doctor and tried to smile.

"Your body has taken all it can endure – it's time to die," he said with a distraught, sad expression on his face.

"Don't, Van. Don't be sorry," I told him. "I'm going to be out of this hell soon and I'll be free. It's official and I'm glad."

"Delores, I would do anything in the world to make you well and I can't do a thing."

Then, after a long pause, he added, "Even the tissues in your back are shredding."

He explained that some of the muscles in my back had dropped down and caused my bowels to cease functioning. My body was preparing for death.

He smiled, squeezed my hand, and left the room.

During the next few days, I tried to adjust to the idea of dying.

After that, we carefully planned my funeral. I tagged my jewelry and the little things I wanted to leave to my loved ones,

About all there was left for me to do was wait.

Days of Anguish

2

In 1958 before Bill moved us to Texas God gave us a baby. We already had our teenage son Doug but never dreamed our family would increase.

While we were living in Portland, God worked our circumstances that allowed me to become acquainted with a certain woman.

About 2 a.m. one morning she called on the phone and was crying.

"Delores, I'm going to have a baby," she said, sobbing.

Well, that's not so bad," I replied. "It happens all the time."

"But I can't keep it – I can't raise the child," she said. "I want the child to have the best Christian home I know and that's yours and Bill's. Will you take the baby?"

"Of course we will," I answered.

We talked for another hour then I hung up the phone a prepared to go back to sleep.

"Who was that?" Bill asked.

I told him it was a lady I knew.

"What did she want?"

"To give us a baby."

"Oh," he said as he turned over in bed to go back to sleep.

A few minutes later he raised up in bed and yelled, "What did you say?"

"Forget it, Bill, she just found out she's pregnant and wants us to take the baby but she'll decide to keep it."

But from that time on, the baby was ours.

When my friend talked about the child she was carrying, she always referred to it as "your baby." She completely disassociated herself from it for she knew she couldn't keep it.

Before the baby was born, we knew the judge would grant the adoption because a foster child had done so well in our home.

The baby was such a precious little fellow. We immediately loved him as our own.

We named him Christopher which means "Christ bearer."

That name was so appropriate for he became an instrument of God's light in my life.

Soon after he was born Bill decided we would move to Arlington, Texas.

When we arrived there, the first thing we did was find a doctor and schedule an appointment to see him for an examination. He carefully reviewed my medical history and through the X-rays confirmed the current fusion had not only broken but had shattered. Hence, he placed me on an experimental medication for seven months hoping it would mend.

Throughout the next seven months my friends and neighbors helped take care of Chris and I thanked God for them.

Our merciful Lord who hears and answers our

prayers always gave me exactly what I asked of him.

Unfortunately, at that time in my life I knew nothing about God's promises to heal my body.

I had grown up in church, read the Bible, and taught Sunday school for many years. I was not dumb just blind to what God's Word says about healing.

Now there was the added grief of having a child barely a year old and not being able to care for him.

That's when I began to question God.

"God why? Why did you give this child to us? He has spent three months with grandparents he didn't even know and all the while crying for me and not understanding why I deserted him."

But that was only the beginning for the little boy. He would have to endure more years of that kind of life.

There were so many people taking care of him and telling him what to do and each of them had different ideas of what was best for him. He didn't understand what was happening and became nervous, anxious, and uncertain of both himself and Bill and me. Misery was all he knew during the first five years of his life. Every day he saw his mother in bed always suffering with bottles of pills everywhere. And during that time, he never saw me without the body cast.

I, too, became uncertain and repeatedly asked, "God, where are you?"

As the years passed, we worked out some semblance of a normal family life. I could get out of bed at times and Bill was able to go to work.

Betty, a Japanese lady, was our good friend and neighbor. She spent a lot of time with Chris and me.

She taught him to draw pictures and he enjoyed it.

With her quiet, loving nature, she was such a blessing to us.

As my pain grew worse my doctor started injections in my spine.

On certain occasions when we arrived at the doctor's office for our appointments, his nurse would come out to the parking lot to give me a shot of Demerol. That would settle me down enough to get me out of the car and into the office.

One day I realized my legs were getting numb. I didn't tell Bill about it for I knew that our time of family stability was just about over.

The pain was so bad Bill improvised a bed for me.

He took an old army cot, stripped it, and used webbing in such a way that my spine was as free as possible not touching anything.

The new bed along with the increased shots up and down my spinal area provided some comfort but even that didn't last.

My life was a vicious cycle of pain, trips to the hospital, and medical bills, my concern for Chris, and day-by-day wondering how long I could endure.

One day in 1975 after my last hospital visit, I was talking to Betty about dying.

"You have big power in you," she said in broken English. "I don't understand it but you'll not die."

I was too exhausted to tell her that all I wanted was to go on to heaven and be free from all the suffering,

Our Methodist minister was no longer coming to see me. But in all fairness who wouldn't grow weary of seeing me in my hopeless condition?

A Presbyterian minister did visit me regularly and

tried to bring as much comfort to me as possible. He became my new pastor and I wanted him to preach my funeral.

But thoughts of Chris kept flashing through my mind and I prayed, "God, just one more year and perhaps he will be old enough to survive losing his mother."

I kept getting what I prayed for – one more year at a time. As a matter of fact, I always received what I asked from God. But that was all I knew to ask from him.

There were times when my fighting for life was so painful and seemed so futile. But the thought of my young Chris getting ready to lose his mother put some fight back in me.

I knew my fight was just about over.

I remembered that during one of my frontal surgeries my heart stopped. But the doctors revived me.

"Why didn't I die?" I wondered.

Other times I would think, "I'm caught in a trap. I cannot live in this pain and I can't die."

Of course, the answer was simple – Jesus heals. But no one told me about that. I believed the Lord for my salvation and knew he would help me over the rough places during my illness but I knew nothing about healing.

The churches we attended taught that miraculous healing was only for the time Jesus was here on earth and the Apostolic Age and that today healing comes only through medicine, surgery and doctors.

"Only fanatics believe in any other healing," they

explained to me.

The result? I wasn't healed.

The deterioration became worse and the pain more severe as the osteoporosis spread up my spine, skipped three vertebrae, spread across my shoulders, and into my neck.

It even affected my fingers and wrists. I could no longer pick up even the lightest object without feeling pain. And at times my wrists would come out of their joints.

The doctors taught Bill how to put them back in place. But I had to wear an elastic bandage around them for days.

One day I fell causing excruciating pain. After the fall, I could no longer hold my head up so the doctors prescribed a large Queen Anne (medical) collar for me.

During those days of terrible discontent, we tried as a family to spend one hour each day together in the den in our home talking, laughing, even playing games – or at least trying to play games. Then later Bill would carry me back to bed.

Chris lived with painful emotions that nearly destroyed him as he watched me slowly dying.

Each afternoon when he returned home from school, he would shout "Mother" not knowing if I had made it through another day.

If I was asleep and didn't immediately answer him, he panicked, screamed, and ran through the house trying to find me.

Once I remained in the hospital for so long, he thought I had died and Bill had not told him.

When they brought me home, he almost collapsed

for he had made up his mind he would never see me again.

His was a mother he had never seen out of a body cast, who hardly ever visited his school, a mother he couldn't hug for fear he might hurt her or cause her more pain, and a mother who soon would be leaving him forever.

One day when a minister came to visit, I told him, "I don't understand why God would let a little boy suffer like this?"

The minister reflected on my question, then replied, "Delores, look at the strength he's giving the little boy."

"Dear Lord!" I thought. "How much strength does a little boy need? How much sickness does he need to see and how much does he have to suffer to be strong?"

There were times when my heart became so weak I feared it might stop beating. Immediately, I would think, "This is it."

Then I would take a couple of deep breaths and it would start beating regularly again. I dreaded the return of the pounding in my chest for I so wanted to die.

At times I held my breath for long periods of time. I thought if I held my breath long enough my heart would stop. But always, just before it stopped, the thought of a motherless Chris flashed through my mind and I started breathing again.

One evening I heard Chris crying. I shuffled into his room to find out what was wrong.

He looked up at me with tears in his eyes and said, "You're dying, aren't you, Mother?"

"Yes, Chris, but everyone dies."

"No, I mean you're dying now."

"Yes, I am," I answered hesitantly. "Chris, if you cry that's all we'll remember. But if we try to enjoy each day there will be some happy memories."

He didn't understand.

"Can't you be happy for me? It's time for me to go to Heaven where I will no longer be sick and in pain. Can't you be happy for that?"

"But what about me?" he asked. "What is going to happen to me? How will I feel when I come home from school and you are not here?"

His question stunned me and it bothered me that I could say nothing that would give him strength and courage.

The thought occurred to me that I could say, "Chris, you can pray."

But he had prayed for me from the time Bill and I first taught him to pray and hadn't seen any answers.

He was like a wound-up spring and so nervous he bit his fingernails to the quick.

I was afraid that when I died, he would snap emotionally and no one would be able to put him back together.

"God, please show me something that will save Chris. Show me that when I'm gone, he will be alright," I prayed

Some days later, I broke down and wept, crying out to God, "You've got to give me some assurance Chris will not fall apart."

There had been times when I would dump a bunch of pills in my hand thinking if I took them all at once I could end my useless, helpless life. But the thought of

Chris being alone always stopped me.

"How could he accept a suicide in addition to all the other heartaches he had to endure? So, I placed the pills back in the bottle.

Even in the midst of the terrible anguish concerning Chris – and wracking pain so intense the painkillers would bring no relief -- God was good to me.

Some days I would rise above the pain by imagining myself sitting on a mountaintop looking down at a little ribbon of a river flowing through the valley. Or sitting on a piece of driftwood watching the waves coming in and listening to the sounds of the sea.

I could even see colorful wildflowers growing on my imaginary mountain.

As my mind wandered to the faraway places my pain would go away at least for a while.

When you are bedfast, you learn to appreciate little things that seem relatively unimportant in a busy world: a child laughing, a baby crying, or a teenager walking carefree down the street.

Children often are afraid of the grotesque including a strange-looking lady in a body cast that can't run and play with them. Yet I rarely met a child that was afraid to come near me. Instead, children would come up and ask to touch the cast.

One child rapped on my cast and asked, "Are you in there?" making a joyful game out of it.

It made me laugh.

Friends came to visit me nearly every day. Some would come once and never return, unable to cope with seeing me in such pain. Some people can't handle another person's lengthy illness for they go through so much with you it drains their emotions.

During those final days I just settled back and waited hoping the end would come soon.

Strange and Wonderful Ways   3

One Sunday morning God sent a woman named Velma Despain to see me.

Her daughter Gail Bond lived near us and often helped take care of me.

Gail asked her mother to stay away from me. She belonged to the Assemblies of God church and people thought she was a little weird.

"I don't want you bothering Delores, she is too sick," Gail told her mother one day.

However, on that particular Sunday, Velma came to our home and Bill brought her to my bedroom.

I had been having church in bed that morning watching a worship service on television.

Even before we had a chance to exchange pleasantries, Velma walked over to the television and switched channels.

Startled, I glanced at the television and saw a woman seemingly floating out onto the stage in a flowing gown, saying very dramatically, "I believe in miracles."

I took one look at the rather strange-looking woman who invaded the relative quiet of my bedroom via the television screen and somewhat caustically asked, "Who's that?"

Velma smiled and replied, "That's Kathryn

Kuhlman."

"Turn her off!"

"Don't you ever watch her program?"

"No, turn her off!"

When I was young, my family lived in Johnstown, Pennsylvania, and I knew all about Kathryn Kuhlman the so-called faith-healer since her headquarters were in Pittsburg. We referred to her as "That kook who says she heals people."

Newspapers and doctors had exposed her and everyone knew she was a fake.

Once when she came to the Johnstown area for one of her healing meetings our Methodist minister told us to stay away from her meetings and, being good Methodists, our family stayed away.

When Velma saw that I was upset she reached over and changed the channel and I felt an immediate sense of relief.

"Why don't you watch Kathryn Kuhlman?"

"Because I don't like her."

Although I was being rude, Velma kept smiling.

She didn't say another word until it was time for her to return home.

"Goodbye," she said as she walked toward the door. Then she turned, looked me straight in the eye, and asked, "What if you are closing the door to God?"

"By not watching Kathryn Kuhlman? That's ridiculous!" I laughed.

Velma left the room but her question troubled even disturbed me. After all I was begging God to give me an answer about Chris.

That very day, bewildered by Velma's troublesome

question, I prayed and said, "God, if I can open a door by watching Kathryn Kuhlman, I'll do it. But please tell me otherwise I don't want to watch her."

Sometime later I realized my prayer was a turning point. It was the first time I had told God that I needed to hear from him.

Up to that time my prayers had always been like other people's, something like, "God, if it's your will," or "God, I'm having another surgery and sure need your help."

How many ministers, through the years, prayed simple prayers for me like, "Lord, give Delores the strength to endure."

And endure I did.

During the next two days I prayed about whether to watch the Kathryn Kuhlman television program yet I received no answer.

I thought the windows of Heaven were closed.

Since I heard nothing from God on the matter, I decided it wasn't necessary to watch her program.

But God sneaked up on me.

Having undergone two percutaneous cordotomies I had no control over my body functions. Hence, I never knew when I needed to use the bathroom.

I set up a schedule to remind me to go at certain times. But often during the night I would have an accident and would wake up in a wet bed.

One morning I woke up and the bed was completely dry. I couldn't understand why.

Since Gail, who always helped me to the bathroom, had not yet arrived, I decided to go by myself.

Bill erected a Monkey Bar over my bed and from

time to time I used it to move around a little. That morning, I grabbed the bar and tried to pull myself up into a sitting position so I could go to the bathroom.

Suddenly a pain hit my shoulder and shot through my neck and into my head.

I thought my brain had exploded.

In great agony I fell back down in the bed.

But as I fell, I distinctly heard a clear voice say the words, *Kathryn Kuhlman*. I well remember I heard only her name and nothing else.

That really threw me for a loop.

I yelled, "Gail!" but she didn't answer.

A few minutes later, Gail walked into my bedroom, looked at me and said, "You're awfully quiet."

"Gail, were you here a few minutes ago?"

"No,"

"I heard someone say Kathryn Kuhlman's name."

"You told God if it was his will, you would watch her program, perhaps you should."

"Maybe I will."

The next day Gail's mother Velma came to see me again.

Actually, that day she was leaving for California but stopped by to see how I was doing.

"Delores, Kathryn Kuhlman is going to be in Dallas at the end of the month," she informed me. "If you are interested in going to see her here are the phone numbers to call for reservations."

Miss Kuhlman was invited to be the featured speaker for the United Methodist Church Conference on the Holy Spirit in the Dallas Convention Center.

I took the piece of paper with the phone numbers,

all the time thinking, "Why am I doing this? I won't even be alive at the end of the month. Velma is really flaky."

After she left, I picked up the phone, called the number she had given me, and ordered two tickets.

However, the tickets never came.

The doctor had me so doped up on pain medications, I didn't even realize the tickets never arrived.

"Perhaps the people in the ticket office asked me to send a check and I didn't remember," I thought when I finally discovered I had not received the tickets.

In August of 1975, several of my family members and friends came to see me for a last visit. Since we had so many visitors in our home and because I didn't know one day from another, I didn't watch Kathryn Kuhlman's programs for two weeks.

Those were such difficult days and it took all my strength just to hang on to life.

Then God started moving again.

By the end of the month, I was barely alive and finally realized I had not received the tickets.

"Oh well, God didn't want me to go, anyway," I decided.

At that time in my life I didn't realize that we have an enemy who tries to stop us from doing those things God wants us to do.

A few days later for some unknown reason Velma's husband called her in California and told her to come home.

When she asked why, he said, "I just want you to come home tomorrow."

Although the strong-willed Velma was fuming, she

returned home and Gail met her at the airport.

The next morning, Velma happened to call her eighty-three-year-old Aunt Ruth in Dallas.

"Did Delores get to go hear Kathryn Kuhlman?" her aunt asked.

Velma, who had told her aunt about my illness, said, "No."

"I have one ticket for tonight and I know its hers," her aunt said.

Velma's elderly aunt had wanted to call me to offer me the ticket but didn't know my last name.

Although it didn't dawn on me at the time, one thing was very clear: Velma came home from California in order for me to get that ticket and attend the conference on the Holy Spirit.

God was working through others in order to get me where he wanted me.

An amazing detail was that the meeting for which Aunt Ruth gave me a ticket was for the Methodist conference. However, the tickets I ordered were for the meeting of the Full Gospel Businessmen's conference also in Dallas.

Had I attended the men's meeting and seen someone with hand lifted in praise or who shouted "Hallelujah," I would have split the door wide open getting out of there. To me fanaticism has no place in the church or among Christians.

However, I knew the Methodist meeting would be quiet and orderly and no one would get excited or carried away.

Once I knew I had the ticket, I had to tell Bill I wanted to go to the meeting.

I asked him to come into the bedroom and said, "Bill, I've got to go to Dallas to hear Kathryn Kuhlman."

He looked at me rather strangely and asked, "Why?"

"Because I'm going to learn something that I need to know to help Chris."

Bill, always the thinker, always full of logic, asked, "How are you going to get there?"

"Gail will take me."

He reluctantly agreed.

On Saturday night Gail helped him get me ready for the ride from Arlington to Dallas.

Before we left, he told Gail, "Now when you get there, she won't be able to go inside so just turn around and bring her home."

He realized that it would be too painful for me to get out of the car, go into the Convention Center, find a seat, and sit through the meeting.

Just as we were leaving, Chris came into the bedroom and said, "Mother, where are you going?"

"Chris, I have to go to Dallas."

"What for?"

"To hear a woman speak."

"You must really like her."

"No, I don't like her at all."

"Then why are you going?"

"Because God is going to teach me something I need to know for you."

"Mother, why don't you like her?"

"She's a woman I know about from Pennsylvania and she says she heals people."

"Mother, you're going to be healed."

Chris was so excited his face glowed. However, I

felt he should not have said I was going to be healed. I wanted to correct him so he wouldn't build up his hopes and then be disappointed when I returned home sick.

"Chris, come here and sit down," I said and he obediently sat down on the side of the bed. "Healings do not happen anymore. There were healings when Jesus was here and later with the disciples and apostles but they do not take place today. I don't want you thinking I'm coming home any different that I am now."

Then I added, "But I'm going to learn something your dad and I need to know to help you."

"Yes ma'am," he said.

Then it was time to go.

Bill carried me to the car and laid me down in the back seat where, earlier, he had made a bed of blankets and pillows.

The trip to Dallas took twenty-five minutes. Although my pain was severe, the hope of hearing something from God to leave with Chris when I died helped me bear the pain.

We arrived at the Dallas Convention Center and Gail drove up to the entrance.

She turned around to me in the back seat and asked, "Can you get out?"

"No," I replied.

I was so weak I could hardly keep my senses let alone try to go into an auditorium.

"Well, we'll just go back home," Gail said with a sound of relief in her voice.

Suddenly the back door of the car opened and a man stood there looking at me.

"Let me help you,' he said

He reached inside the back seat and lifted me up and out of the car.

He told Gail to park the car and said he would take care of me.

"I'll take her to the lobby and wait for you there," he said.

When Gail entered the lobby, the kind man helped me shuffle into the auditorium where he located our seats and helped me sit down. Although he tried to make me comfortable, it wasn't possible.

I asked him if he would bring me a cup of water so I could take my pain pills.

He did.

4
Rise and Be Healed

The appearance of Kathryn Kuhlman was the big event of the Methodist Conference that Saturday night of Aug. 30, 1975.

She just floated out on the stage wearing a long, flowing gown and, with a big smile on her face, dramatically said, "I believe in miracles!"

I took one look at her up on the stage, and said, "Dear Lord, what am I doing here?"

All of my negative feelings about her rose up within me. I didn't even want to be in the same auditorium with her.

Then an inner voice spoke to me, "Now you came here to learn something. You don't have to look at her to learn it."

"Sure," I thought," I won't learn anything by watching her."

Besides, I had on a neck brace and a body cast and couldn't hold up my head.

I managed a glance at her a couple of times during the evening.

But oh, did I learn something that night!

As she spoke, she introduced me to the God I didn't know. She talked about the Holy Spirit and even called it he,

"He is the third person of the Trinity," she said.

"Why does she keep calling the Holy Spirit he?" I asked myself.

She told the packed audience in the Convention Center that night that if we were still referring to the Holy Spirit as it, we really didn't know him.

While she spoke of the Holy Spirit coming to be with us and explained that he was the very presence of God with us doing the work Jesus did, I knew his presence for the first time in my life. I felt it all around me. I thought that if I were to reach out my hand, I could have touched him.

Although I don't remember exactly what Kathryn Kuhlman said that evening it was something like this: "Do you know him? If you don't know him, why? Jesus was so certain of the Holy Spirit and the work he would do. He knew the Holy Spirit would come to continue his work and once here promised never to leave or forsake you."

I was afraid but I knew I was feeling the presence of God.

As I became aware I was meeting God in the service that night, I found myself open to him. He was not sitting way up on his throne somewhere in the heavens. He was right there with me.

As I sat there listening to the message, the Lord opened up my mind and told me what I needed to know for Chris.

I closed my eyes hoping to shut out everything but the awareness of him. Behind my closed eyes I saw Chris standing on our front porch and he was not alone. There was a man standing beside him.

Then I heard the man speak, saying, "Tell Chris he

need never walk into the house alone. Tell him to close his eyes and picture Jesus, then reach out and take my hand. I'll always walk with him. My name is Holy Spirit."

I was absolutely sure I heard the Lord speak to me. He gave me the answer to what would become of Chris and the other members of my family when I would be gone.

"Lord, it is so simple," I said. "Please don't let me forget this before I get home."

I worried I might forget everything that happened that night because of the heavy doses of medications I was taking.

"That's what I came to learn and now I'm ready to go home," I said to Gail as joy filled my heart. "Oh, thank you Lord. Chris will never be alone. You will always be with him."

Although I received an intimate revelation, by this time my head was aching so badly it actually felt like it would explode.

"I wish she would stop speaking so we can go home."

In what seemed like an answer to my prayer, she stopped speaking and started praying.

"Lord, you are so good, it's just about over, "I thought

Every part of me that could hurt was hurting. My body was throbbing with pain so intense I wanted to scream."

Then Kathryn Kuhlman stopped praying, and said, "Someone out there just had a deaf ear opened. If you'll come up here, you'll receive your healing."

A man stood up and walked toward the platform and up the stairs to her. Several others followed him.

She walked around behind the man and, in her stage whisper (which was almost as loud as my voice) said, "Can you hear me?"

"Sure, he can hear her, I can hear her clear back here," I said.

The man replied, "Yes, I can hear you!"

"Well, that's just great, everyone in here can hear you," I thought, not believing the man had been deaf. "Why shouldn't he hear you?"

Several of the other people who followed the man up onto the platform started jumping up and down, each saying, "I can hear! I can hear!"

I wondered what was going on.

Then Kathryn walked up in front of one of the men and, when she touched him, he fell to the floor.

I couldn't believe my eyes.

"Why did she knock him down?"

Then she went to all the other people who had answered the call to be healed and one by one knocked them down.

When she approached a really large man, I thought, "She won't be able to knock him down?"

But when she touched him, he hit the floor.

"She should not have been able to knock that big man down," I reasoned. "Oh, I know, pressure points, she's hitting pressure points."

Right at that point a voice said to me, "Get out of here, she's making a mockery of God. Why does God allow her to do that?"

"That's right," I agreed. "Here she introduced me to the living God and now she has a sideshow going on up on the platform."

Again, the voice spoke to me and said, "Get out of here."

I turned to Gail and said, "Let's go home."

"God, let me leave here and don't let any of them nab me," I prayed.

Suddenly I realized the tops of my leg were on fire and so painful I had to bite my lips.

I clasped my legs together to keep from screaming.

I waited for Gail to help me get out of that crazy place.

Then someone said to me, "Why are you wearing the neck brace?"

I looked around and there was a man crouched down by my seat.

"I have a bad neck," I answered and turned away from him.

"Is something happening to you?" he asked.

"Yes, my legs are burning like fire."

"Would you like to walk with me?"

"Yes, get me out of here."

He helped me stand up.

In my heart, I knew the Lord sent the man to get me out of that place.

Realizing I couldn't walk, he asked, "How can I help you?"

"If you put your arm around me, I can shuffle."

I was so pleased the man was helping me get away from Kathryn Kuhlman.

As I shuffled along, he asked me some questions.

Questions about my condition always annoyed me and I usually had a smart answer. When you are an invalid, you become quite clever answering questions.

"Have you had surgery?" he asked,

"I've had four fusions and two percutaneous cordotomies," I replied.

When I used the medical term percutaneous cordotomies, it usually shut people up for good.

He stopped, turned me around to face him, and said, "You've had two percutaneous cordotomies and your legs are burning. Isn't that rather strange?"

"Yes," I answered and decided not to say anything more to him.

He led me to the door that opened into the lobby as I used my cane to steady myself and shuffle along.

When we reached the door, he said, "You don't know what is happening to you but you can take off your cast if you want to."

"My God! These people are dangerous," I thought, "Here's a man I have never seen in my life telling me I can take off my cast."

I turned to him to say, "You shouldn't do this to people."

But when I looked him in the face the words wouldn't come out.

He looked down at me again and said, "You can take off the cast if you want to."

I didn't answer.

"Do you want to take off the cast?" he repeated.

"I've been in this cast for fifteen years and I'm dying," I answered. "Certainly, I want to take it off."

The next thing I knew he took me to the women's room where I leaned against the wall and began ripping off my cast.

Gail followed me into the room and, when she saw

me taking off the cast, said, "Delores, what in the world are you doing?"

"Taking off my cast."

"Why, do you feel different?"

"No."

"Then why are you taking it off," she asked. "Delores, this isn't like you."

Then I started putting my cast back on again.

The man walked to the door and said, "Come on. What are you waiting for?"

I listened to what he said and started ripping the cast off again

When I was completely free of the cast, I handed it to Gail and said, "Get me back out there to that man."

He and an usher helped me back into the auditorium.

As he helped me sit down, Kathryn called out to him, "What do you have there, Doctor?"

"I have a spine," he replied.

"Oh, he's a doctor. That's why he knows what a cordotomy is."

"Bring her up here," Kathryn said

As the doctor and one of the ushers escorted me to the stage I thought, "Oh dear God, they are going to put me in the sideshow."

I was somewhat relieved that no one in the audience knew me.

They helped me across the platform to where Kathryn was standing. She looked me in the face and said, "You're in a lot of pain, aren't you?"

"Yes," I replied, thinking anyone should be able to tell from the way I looked that I was in pain.

"Walk to the back of the stage," she ordered me.

"She can't, Kathryn, she has no support," the doctor informed her.

"Oh, Doctor, tell me what's wrong with her."

The doctor went to the microphone.

He told the three thousand people assembled in the auditorium that surgeons had performed four spinal fusions and two percutaneous cordotomies on me. He also explained that although I was not supposed to feel anything in my legs they were burning.

While the doctor was speaking, two other men held me up in order to keep me from falling.

Kathryn turned around, moved closer to me, and repeated, "Now, walk to the back of the stage."

Then she just stood there with her hands on her sides.

"She's not only weird, she apparently didn't hear what the doctor said about me."

What a sight I must have been. I did not have my cast or brace to support me, my body was twisted, one of my legs was nearly an inch shorter than the other, my spine was deteriorated, and my body bent over, yet this woman was asking me to walk to the back of the stage.

Again, she said, "Walk."

I knew she was going to stand there looking at me her hands on her sides until I did something and I wondered if we were going to stand there just looking at one another the rest of the evening in front of three thousand people.

I decided to push my right foot out to show her I couldn't walk. When I put my foot out, it came up off the floor for the first time in years. When I put my foot back down, I thought I could feel the floor.

But an inner voice told me, "No, you don't feel the floor."

All I knew for certain was that my foot stepped out further than I expected or intended.

During that time a pastor was holding me up and I knew if he let go, I would fall flat on my face for I couldn't balance myself.

Then I decided to put my other foot out in front of me. I put it out and it came up off the floor and back down.

"I do feel the floor but my mind kept saying, 'No, you don't feel the floor. Get out of here, this is no place for you.'"

Then I felt my pants rubbing against the tops of my legs and I started getting some feeling in my fingertips for the first time since I had my first cordotomy five years earlier.

I began to scream, "I can feel! I can feel!"

But my screams of joy didn't seem to mean a thing to Kathryn even though I hadn't walked without help in five years but was there running around on the stage!

A third time she ordered me to walk to the back of the stage and I don't remember what happened after that.

Those who witnessed the miracle said I took off running to the back of the stage then back to Kathryn.

"Now, bend over," she said.

Since my fusions were above my waist, I hadn't been able to do so for years. The tissues in my back were shredding, my shoulder was so deteriorated if I even moved it, the agony was unbearable

Yet, there she was, telling me to bend over.

Just to show her I could bend over only a little, I started to bend over and suddenly realized my shoulders were loose and moving. I kept bending until I touched the floor.

When I rose up, she said, "Do it again."

I did, but this time I placed my hands flat on the floor.

Then she ordered me to twist.

I knew I couldn't twist because of the fusions but I decided to try. I gingerly started twisting and found complete flexibility in my upper body.

By then feeling was coming back into my whole body.

"Now, do you have any pain?" she asked.

"No," I replied.

I kept telling her that I could feel and then it dawned on me that the pain was gone.

Suddenly she reached out her hand and touched me.

I grabbed the podium as visions of her knocking down those big, strong men danced through my mind.

When they picked me up off the floor, I wondered what had happened.

She looked at me and said, "I think God would like for you to have a double dose."

She touched me and I fell to the floor again.

When I awakened and stood, Kathryn shook her finger at me and said, "That is the power of the Holy Spirit and don't you forget it! Now you have work to do."

Those who witnessed the miracle that night said it

took only fifteen minutes for God to release me from the chains of sickness that had bound me for 19 ½ years.

I could never have imagined myself, a dying cripple that knew nothing of healing leaving home at six o'clock in the evening and returning home completely healed at two o'clock the next morning.

But, let me tell you, that's how God works. He does everything first class and he did so for me.

I later learned that the doctor who picked me out of the three thousand people assembled in the Convention Center that evening was Dr. Richard Owellen of Johns Hopkins Medical School in Baltimore, Maryland. He was a faithful follower of Kathryn Kuhlman's ministry.

He previously had been a member of a group of doctors who were quite critical of her and traveled to her meetings to find something to discredit her ministry.

However, over time after observing her ministry he became convinced that it was of God and that she was called to minister healing to the people.

Following a miraculous experience in his own life, he received the gift of knowledge from the Holy Spirit.

He began traveling to various Kuhlman meetings no longer to discredit her but to help her.

Through the gift of knowledge, he often knew when someone in the audience was being healed. Then God would lead him directly to that person.

That was what led him to me that night in Dallas.

On the morning of the Saturday when I was healed, Dr. Owellen called one of Kathryn's aides to inquire about the evening service.

The aide told him that Kathryn would minister at the Methodist conference and had been asked to speak on the Holy Spirit. But they specifically said they didn't want any healing ministry.

The doctor told the aide he wouldn't be attending the Saturday night meeting for he was scheduled to attend a professional meeting in another city.

But God spoke to him and told him to go to Dallas.

When he arrived, one of Kathryn's aides asked him, "What are you doing here?"

"The Lord sent me," he replied.

The doctor told me later that he had been sitting up on the platform during the early portion of the service. Then he got up and walked down a long aisle in the auditorium and then another. He didn't stop walking until he got to me.

I thought he had picked me out of the crowd but God led him to me and he got there just as I was trying to get away from the place.

I was also told that I probably would not have received my healing had it not been for the doctor. If I had left the meeting believing as I did that God no longer healed people and thinking my legs were burning because of the cast rubbing against them I might never have been healed.

So sad to think that I would have left the auditorium still dying and burdened with all the medical illnesses in which Satan had trapped me.

Instead, I walked away from the stage completely healed.

Praise be to God!

After the service concluded, many of the people

were praising God. Several of them, greatly excited over my healing, wished me well and said they would be praying for me.

As Gail and I prepared to leave the Convention Center, Dr. Owellen said, "Delores, I have to caution you about something. Satan will try to tell you that you have not been healed.

I didn't understand what the doctor was saying. I never talked about Satan and he didn't bother me or my family. He lived in hell. Or that was what I thought.

Gail and I walked out of the auditorium toward our parked car carrying my cast and neck brace. I threw them into the back seat with the pillows and blankets, opened the front door, and spryly sat down inside.

I looked over at Gail and saw her face was white as a sheet for she was unable to process the miracle she had seen with her own eyes.

She broke the silence.

"What are you going to tell Bill?"

"I don't know."

Gail realized I had a real problem ahead.

"Please put your cast on," she implored me.

"No! I feel great!"

Surges of energy coursed through my body giving me strength that would go up and down my body. Each time it made a full circle I became stronger.

Can you imagine what it must have been like for Gail who had cared for me all those years to see me completely healed? Or can you imagine what it would be like for Bill and Chris to see me come home a new person?

When we arrived back at Gail's home, which was

near ours, she pulled into the driveway and abruptly said, "I'll see you tomorrow."

Then she jumped out of the car and ran toward her house.

"Oh, no! What am I going to tell Bill?" I called to her.

"I can't help you. Good night."

Chris watched us pull into Gail's driveway.

When I stepped out of the car, he came running from across the street screaming, "Mother, you were healed! You were healed!"

That Sunday morning was the first time in his fourteen years Chris had seen me get out of a car by myself.

Still screaming, he picked me up and swung me round and round.

All those years of my illness, Chris had to be careful to gently touch me

But now he was swinging me around in the middle of the street at 2 a.m. in the morning yelling at the top of his lungs.

Then he picked me up and carried me toward our house.

Bill had been waiting on the front porch for my return home but when he saw Chris carrying me toward the house, he was stunned and went back into the house.

Chris continued screaming. I tried to quiet him down thinking he would awaken the neighbors.

But he didn't and kept screaming and shouting until he carried me into the house.

"Mother, can we go to church together tomorrow, our whole family?" he asked.

Bill looked at me rather skeptically and asked, "Where's your cast?"

"In the car," I replied.

Seeing the shock on his face, I said, "Bill, I'm alright."

I began moving my head back and forth to show him my neck was free. Then I bent over and touch my hands to the floor.

"And I can feel!" I said gleefully clenching my fist open and shut

Staring at me in disbelief, Bill said, "Okay, you can feel, now let's go to bed."

For the first time in many years, I went to bed without taking any pills. I fell into a deep sleep and slept like a baby all night.

But Bill never went to bed. He stayed awake trying to understand what he was seeing with his eyes but could not understand.

To some people the amazing events of that evening might have been the beautiful ending to a sad story. But it wasn't.

It was the beginning of a nightmare for Bill and me.

Good Times, Bad Times   5

I woke up the next morning feeling great. I went to the bathroom to take a shower by myself for the first time in years.

The first thing I did when I got to the bathroom was to tear a bandage off my back. There had been an open draining sore on my back for the past seven months.

Then I stepped into the shower and gave my seventy-three-pound body the scrubbing of its life.

After drying off with a towel – all by myself – I went to the kitchen to fix some breakfast.

Bill, who had been sitting in the den most of the night, came into the kitchen, stared at me and asked, "What are you doing?"

"I'm going to eat something, then we're going to church."

"Hm," he muttered and said nothing more.

Chris jumped up and down when I told him we were going to church.

"Do you really feel like going to church?" Bill asked.

"Yes, Bill, I feel great."

"Okay, we'll go."

He went to the bedroom and started dressing for church.

When I walked in, he said, "Let's dress the sore on your back."

"All right."

He prepared the necessary bandages but when I turned around for him to apply them, Bill said, "The sore is scarred over."

I swung around and looked at his pale face. We both were stunned.

When I looked at my back in the mirror indeed the sore was gone. All that remained was a small white scar. It looked like an old scar except it appeared someone had taken a pin and drawn blood in a circle leaving a red ring around it.

Bill sighed and went back to the bedroom

Suddenly it dawned on me we were living out something that neither of us understood.

Overnight God transformed me from a hopeless, helpless invalid to a perfectly well, energetic woman. Who could possibly understand such a thing?

I was so jubilant and to see the joy on Chris's face caused great happiness to well up within me.

However, Bill was silent that Sunday morning as we drove toward the Presbyterian Church.

He later told me he had made up his mind that if whatever happened to me lasted only one or two days it would be worth it and whatever the outcome, we would try to be happy.

Bill was a structural steel inspector but had a minor in psychology in college and that background kept him trying to understand what had happened to me.

"Is it just some kind of illusion?" he wondered. "Or was she hypnotized?"

Whatever it was he decided to accept it for as long as it lasted and, if I were to suddenly collapse, he would deal with it.

We walked into church and learned the pastor was out of town and none of the church members recognized me. I decided not to tell any of the church members about my healing until I had discussed it with my doctor.

As we walked out of the church, I said to Bill, "Let's go to Colonial Cafeteria for lunch."

"You sure you feel up to it?"

"I feel great and I'm starved."

"No, I think I should take you home so you can rest."

Of course, there was no way Bill could understand my sudden hunger since for years I had no appetite.

The food in the cafeteria looked so good to me. By the time we had gone through the line there was enough food on my tray to feed all three of us.

I ate cucumbers in vinegar, fried chicken, watermelon, and cherry pie.

Bill just sat and watched me eat.

While sitting there eating in the cafeteria, it finally dawned on me that my years of sickness were over. God really had healed me!

But my dear wonderful Bill kept searching for some rational explanation for what had happened.

Of course there was no natural explanation only a supernatural one. It was just going to take time for him to understand.

That afternoon we decided to go to Mansfield, Texas, to see our thirty-year-old son Doug, his wife Ann, and our grandchildren.

That day I made my first mistake after being healed.

When we drove up to their house, Doug was working

in the yard. He saw our car but of course knew I was too sick to make the trip to Mansfield. So, he presumed I was still at home.

I slipped out of the car and walked over to where he was working.

When he looked around and saw me, it startled him

"Mother, what are you doing here?" he asked

I looked at him, smiled, and asked, "Can you use me on your football team?"

I thought he would appreciate me saying that for he was a coach.

Then I bent over and placed the palms of my hands squarely on the ground.

But I could tell by the look in his face that I should not have approached him that way.

Unexpectedly, Doug couldn't get his breath and I thought he was having a heart attack right there in his front yard.

He began shaking as if he had chills

Bill grabbed him and helped him into the house where he sat down

Our daughter-in-law Ann came outside just in time to see me touch the ground with the palms of my hands.

She screamed, and said, "Mother, what are you doing?"

"It's alright, Ann, I'm healed."

"What do you mean you are healed?" she asked with a trembling voice

"I don't know, but I'm healed. I'm alright now."

During the final stages of my illness Ann often would come to our home in Arlington to dress the sore on my back.

"Mother, let me see the sore," she said.

"Okay," I replied as I lowered my blouse.

"It's healed!" she shouted as she saw only the scar. "What happened?"

I couldn't explain it to her because I didn't understand it. I didn't even know anyone could be healed or anyone who had been healed.

All I could say to Doug and Ann was, "Look, I'm standing here. I feel fine. All the feeling is back in my body."

Doug, still pale and unable to handle the trauma any longer, said, "Mother, I think you had better go home. I'm going to have to take some time to work through this."

So, we went home.

The nightmare had begun,

God healed me during the Labor Day weekend when Bill had a couple of days off from work.

When he went back to work and left me alone in the house, I learned I was completely unprepared to be by myself.

Crazy thoughts ran through my mind.

"I'm still not well," I thought. "My mind is just gone."

I stood in front of a large mirror, looked at myself, and said, "I am healed. Look, I can move my head, bend over, lift my feet, and walk."

My mind needed a lot of convincing to understand what had happened to my body.

One thing that complicated our understanding of the miracle was that neither Bill nor I had ever received any teaching on healing. We had never read a book or heard a sermon on the subject. In the past when we ran across Bible verses on healing, we didn't understand their meaning.

I cried more during the first ten days after my healing than during the long years of my illness and, after the difficult experience with Doug and Ann, I was afraid to tell anyone what had happened to me.

The following Monday night I had an attack on my herniated esophagus. It startled me out of a deep sleep.

I immediately grabbed for a bottle of pills.

"Don't take the pills," a still, small voice inside of me said,

I placed them back on the shelf.

The pain in my esophagus was so intense I knew I had to do something. Sweat poured off my body like water.

"What can I do," I cried out.

"Get up," the quiet voice said.

That seemed strange. Usually when I had such an attack, I would pass out cold if I tried to get up. Then Bill would take me to the hospital cardiac care unit.

"Get up! Now," the voice said again.

"I can't get up," I argued.

"Get up." I heard the voice a third time.

As I began to get out of bed, I said, "If I pass out, it's not my fault."

Sitting there on the edge of the bed, I looked at the clock. It was 11 p.m.

I stood, walked to the bathroom, and sat down. I was all knotted up and shaking from fear and pain.

"I won't have this!" I shouted and then I started getting angry.

"God, I won't have this!" I screamed.

Suddenly I felt like something opened up inside my chest and something came out. The pressure and pain disappeared.

I dried off with a towel and returned to bed weak and drained,

As I sat down on the bed, I noticed it was 11:10 p.m. Although it seemed like hours, the attack lasted only ten minutes.

Sometime later, I discussed the experience with Dr. Richard Casdorph, a Spirit-filled physician. He asked me if I understood what happened during esophagus attack. I told him I did not understand it at all.

He explained I had engaged in spiritual warfare. Satan had tried to put the illness back on me. He added that God would not always protect me as he had done that night. I would have to learn how to combat the evil one using all the spiritual provisions God had made for me.

God placed a covering over me for about a year then stepped back. But I learned to take authority over pain and sickness in the name of Jesus and when I prayed. they always went away.

Everything was so unreal and frightening. Bill and I didn't even discuss what had happened to me. We were sort of pretending that it hadn't happened. Bill did go along with how much I had improved even though he really didn't think it would last.

On Tuesday night when I stepped out of the shower Bill saw my back and his face lit up as he realized it was no longer twisted. I had been twisted and bent with one leg longer than the other. For the first time in our married life he observed that my shoulders and hips were even.

"Something did happen to you," Bill admitted shaking his head still unable to logically understand exactly what had happened.

Also, on that Tuesday I had to deal with strange words going around in my mind. The words first appeared earlier when I first awakened on Sunday morning. I knew they were not Latin or French but that was all I understood about them.

Satan kept telling me I had gone bananas and lost my mind. He would whisper in my ear that the strange words were proof I was going crazy. Over and over, he would lie to me saying, "Well, it really happened. You've lost your mind."

Through the long years of my sickness one of my greatest fears was that I would lose my mind before I died. I really was a ripe candidate for insanity. I had taken so many drugs, had so much surgery, and suffered so much pain that my mind had played a lot of tricks on me. I couldn't even remember things that happened from one hour to the next.

The night I was healed God completely delivered me from the drug addiction which had worried me. I had been led to believe no one could get free of drugs without enduring withdrawal pains.

Yet, I did.

Still, the fear of losing my mind provided Satan with an opening to hit me where I was weak.

He'll take every opportunity to do that to Christians.

My emotions swung like a pendulum back and forth from confidence to fear. I would stand in front of

It's Time To Be Healed

the mirror, bend over, touch the floor, then cry out, "I am healed! I don't understand it, but I am healed!"

But even as I walked down the hallway to the kitchen, I would tell myself I was crazy.

On Wednesday, Bill called my doctor Van, and told him we wanted to see him. He set an appointment.

We walked into the waiting room where I sat down.

That was unusual for in the past I would have been lying down on the sofa while waiting to see the doctor.

Van walked into the waiting room, looked at me, and said, "You're different. What happened?"

"Van, I want you to give me a thorough examination," I told him.

"Your neck or back, your shoulder or what?" he asked.

"Everything."

"Well, all right," he said, a puzzled look on his face.

He took my arm and led me into the examination room just as before.

"You're moving really well," he said.

I wasn't trying to move. I wanted Van to help me.

Before I left the auditorium the night of my healing, Dr. Owellen told me, "Have your doctor check you but don't tell him what happened to you until after a thorough examination."

Van stood me up and said, "Hold her." to his nurse.

They both were careful not to touch my left shoulder because previous X-rays revealed it was deteriorating. While examining me, he began to bend me over a little then stopped.

As I stood up and turned toward him, I saw he was in a daze.

He looked at me and said, "Let me see your sore."

He knew the sore on my back had been draining for several months.

After looking at where the sore had been, he said, "It's healed. What happened to you?"

"No, Van, I want you to continue checking me – everything," I said, not answering his question.

"Okay," he reluctantly replied.

He wanted to place me on the examination table and took my arm to help me stand.

"I can do it by myself, Van."

I easily climbed onto the table.

Van started to turn me over when I said, "I can turn over."

He began touching my spine pressing lightly on my neck at first and then harder.

"This isn't hurting you?"

"No."

Then he ran both hands up and down my spine.

"Your spine is straight," he said in utter disbelief. "Delores, tell me what happened."

"First, finish the examination."

Van reached over and touched my shoulder something he had not done in two years for even a simple touch brought me excruciating pain. As he put pressure on it, he watched to see if I would pull away from him as before.

"I haven't touched your shoulder in two-and-a-half years."

"Van, give me your hand," I told him, reaching toward him.

I took his hand and squeezed it. By this time my

grip was like steel.

Again, he asked, "Delores, what happened to you?"

"We're not finished."

"I guess you want me to use the pin."

"Yes."

"Then lay back and don't look."

He took a pin and stuck my legs, arms, and stomach – all the areas where I'd had no feeling for years only numbness due to the cordotomies.

Unable to endure the curiosity any longer, he said, "Okay, that's it. Tell me what happened. But first let me sit down."

I shared with him – in great detail – all of the events that had taken place the night I was healed.

Van sat with his head down as I related the story of my miraculous healing.

Tears streamed down his face.

"Now, Van, you tell me how this could have happened."

In the back of my mind for some unknown reason I hoped there was some medical explanation for what had happened to me. I guess I was seeking a way out for it was all too much for my mind to comprehend.

I hoped he would say, "Look, Delores, this is what really happened to you" and then give me a rational explanation.

He wiped the tears from his eyes, looked straight at me, and said, "You have work to do for the Lord."

His words made me uneasy for I remembered that Kathryn Kuhlman told me virtually the same thing the night I was healed.

Van wasn't the only one who was amazed.

One day while at work Bill was laughing and joking just having a good time with some of the other men.

His joyful attitude caused his friend Lee to ask him, "Why are you so happy?"

Lee knew of my illness and understood I was dying so he couldn't understand why Bill was laughing and joking with the other men.

"My wife was healed," Bill explained.

"Really! That's great!" Lee exclaimed, a broad grin spreading across his face.

"Do you believe that happened?" Bill asked astonished at Lee's interest.

"Well of course," he said. "Do you think your wife would come to our church and give her testimony?"

When Bill told me about the conversation, I asked, "You told him no didn't you?"

"No."

"You know I won't do that!" I shouted.

Bill didn't answer.

After giving me time to cool down, Bill asked, "What should I tell Lee about your visiting his church to give your testimony about your healing?"

I pondered his question for some time and with a strong inner urging impressing me to accept the invitation I reluctantly agreed to go,

"Okay, I'll go just this one time but don't ever ask me to do it again."

The next Sunday morning Bill, Chris, and I drove to the Foursquare church in Dallas where Lee met us at the door. He ushered us down to the front of the church and introduced us to the pastor.

I was not prepared for what I experienced that

It's Time To Be Healed 63

morning. God really treated me roughly probably because I was being so hard-headed about my healing. I still wanted to use reason and logic to describe and understand what happened to me.

As we were sitting in the church waiting for the service to begin a woman by the name of Brenda came into the church. A little later the pastor announced that she would sing.

She walked to the platform.

"I heard a new song this week and love it," she said. "I want to sing it for you today."

The song was about God's healing power.

At that time, I didn't realize how skeptical I was about everything and my heart was filled with resentment.

When she began to sing about healing, I thought sarcastically, "Boy, this is really a buildup for my testimony."

After some additional worship and praise songs, the pastor introduced me as the woman who was miraculously healed at the Kathryn Kuhlman meeting.

As I walked to the platform Brenda the singer gave a spoken prophecy, the first I had ever heard.

Although the prophecy was given in tongues I heard and understood it in perfect English.

What she said angered and frightened me for she had the audacity to describe my life for the next twenty years and how God was going to use me in his service.

I was holding on to the pulpit getting madder every minute.

"Why is she saying those things about my future?" I asked myself fuming inside. "All these people are hearing what she's saying but they are not true! I'm not going to do all those things.'

I was so uncomfortable and wished that I had not accepted the invitation.

After the prophecy, I struggled through my testimony of my miraculous healing going into great detail about everything that had happened.

After it was over, I really lost it!

The pastor's wife came up to me, grabbed hold of me, and said, "I need a touch from God and just want to hold you."

"Don't hold on to me!" I told her rudely as I backed away in disgust. "I don't have anything for you."

I was furious as we left the church that morning. The experience with the pastor's wife really knocked the props out from under me. I was finished.

"The testimony was fine," Bill said as we drove back to our home in Arlington.

Truthfully, I didn't even remember what I had said. All I remembered was the repulsion of having to speak to that group of believers.

It must have been alright for the pastor who was a very sweet man invited me to come back and speak again even after the way I treated his wife.

I became angrier and angrier.

Then I broke the silence. "Bill, don't ever ask me to do that again! That's it! I don't even want to hear about it!"

Chris sat quietly in the back seat listening intently.

"Why, Mother, what's wrong?"

"What that woman Brenda said – that's what's wrong! Why would she have the nerve to say all those things about my future. She doesn't even know me."

"What did she say?" Bill asked.

Then I really got mad. "What do you mean 'what did she say?'"

Suddenly it dawned on me that neither Bill nor Chris understood what she was saying for she was speaking in tongues. But why did I understand every word of it?

Having had no teaching or experience on the biblical teaching on speaking in tongues once again I thought I was losing my mind.

I began to cry.

After we arrived home, I decided to call the pastor and ask him if he understood Brenda's prophecy. He said he had not understood it but sensed it was personal or me and perhaps the Lord was laying out my ministry for me.

All of the things that were happening were too much for me so I decided to walk away from it all.

The next day Maggie Hartner from Kathryn's ministry called me.

I told her about the experience with the pastor's wife and her wanting to hold me in order to get a touch from God. I also told her about the prophecy.

She said she would discuss it with Kathryn.

"I feel like you shouldn't have been so curt with that woman," Maggie said.

Sometime later, Maggie called again.

"Kathryn said you should point people to Jesus by saying, 'You can't plug into me you must plug into Jesus.'"

That was really good advice.

The following Thursday a beautiful woman who had been in and out of our home for years came for a visit.

I invited her to the dining room, took one look at her, and suddenly it was as though the pages of a pornographic book were turning and I was reading her life story.

Immediately I knew she was a lesbian and presently was in the midst of an affair with another woman.

"Oh, dear God, I'd rather be dead than to see things like this," I thought.

It was sickening, even frightening. I saw scenes of her immoral activities that were sinful and sick. Then suddenly it was over.

There was nothing I knew to do to help her so we just visited and then she departed.

The experience was another episode that convinced me I had lost my mind.

After that experience, I stopped answering the telephone. I didn't want anyone else to come to my house and see the seemingly crazy woman I had become.

At that time, I didn't understand what God was doing in my life.

A few days later Maggie Hartner began calling me every day. I spoke with her but couldn't bring myself to explain what was happening in my life.

To make things worse the people at our Presbyterian church had no understanding of supernatural healing. They didn't even speak publicly of it in the church. Hence, they rejected my healing and that hurt.

There was a woman in the church who had been

very good to visit me during the last stages of my illness. One day she called and asked if we could have lunch together.

"Yes, I would love it," I told her,

We went to a restaurant where she related an incredible story to me that caused me to weep.

"Delores, I know what you're going through," she began then related one of the saddest stories I had ever heard.

"I was a patient in a mental institution after the birth of my child," she said. "The doctors told my husband that I was so mentally sick it would be necessary for me to stay in the institution the rest of my life.

"But there in the hospital Jesus appeared to me and healed me and a short time later I was released to return home."

She had a sad look on her face as she continued the story. "But the people in the church would have nothing to do with me. We had to move here to Arlington where my story would remain a secret. So, I know what you are going through."

The dear lady also pointed out that the rejection from the people in her church almost broke her down again causing her to be on the verge of being recommitted to the mental institution,

"But God held on to me," she added. "We moved here where no one knows anything about me."

After hearing her story, I better understood the rejection I was receiving from the people at our church.

Complicating all the other personal problems I was having my phone rang off the hook.

Kathryn had given my name and address to all the

3,000 present the night I was healed. Many of them wanted to know if my healing was real and whether it had lasted. Others wanted to know how I was feeling and asked lots of other bothersome questions.

During those days Satan tried to take my mind. I would stand in front of a mirror and look at myself. I looked okay but something kept telling me it was only an illusion caused by all the medications I had taken during my illness.

One of the worst fears I carried during the long years of my illness was that the painkillers and tranquilizers would destroy my mind. Now as I stood there looking at myself in the mirror Satan convinced me my mind was gone.

After that I stopped answering the phone. I could no longer tell people I was healed.

But the Lord didn't give up on me. Rather he sent Velma Despain back into my life

She came to our house one day and asked me if I would like to go for a ride.

"Yes, of course," I said for I would do anything to get out of the house and away from the phone.

Velma took me for a ride, alright, right to the church of an Assembly of God preacher.

When we arrived, he welcomed us and invited us into his study.

"Velma said I should meet you," he said. "I've been trying to reach you but couldn't so I just asked God to send you to me."

I was embarrassed to tell him I had not been answering the phone.

Sitting there in the presence of a preacher I had

never seen before gave me the jitters. I wanted to run and hide but decided to stay and listen to him.

"You were baptized when you were healed, weren't you?" he asked.

"No, I was baptized in the Methodist church when I was a child."

At that point he realized I didn't know what he was talking about.

It really blew my mind when he said God revealed to him what happened to me even though he had never ever seen me.

I decided he was as crazy as me.

Then he began asking me some questions.

"Are you saying strange words?"

"No."

"Do you know some things you think you shouldn't know?"

I didn't answer for I didn't want to tell him about the lady who was a lesbian who visited my home.

"You're not saying strange words?"

The second time he asked me that question irritated me.

"No!" I emphatically replied.

"Do you have strange words running around in your head?"

I started to cry.

"Do you know what happened to you?"

"Yes, I've lost my mind," I replied, weeping profusely.

"No, you haven't," the gentle pastor assured me. "You were baptized in the Holy Spirit when you were healed and you received some spiritual gifts.

I gained control of my emotions and listened intently

to what he was saying.

"Do you know about the Holy Spirit?"

"No."

The pastor took his Bible and began to teach me about the Holy Spirit.

He read a passage of Scripture where Jesus told his disciples that he is the baptizer in the Holy Spirit. He also read where Jesus told the disciples to wait until the Holy Spirit came upon them and how they waited obediently until that power fell on them on the day of Pentecost.

He also shared with me how the Apostle Peter empowered by the Holy Spirit began preaching to the Romans without concern for his personal safety because of the boldness he received when the Holy Spirit came upon him.

The kind, patient pastor also taught me about the gifts and fruit of the Spirit.

"But those things are not for today and don't happen anymore," I said.

"What do you think happened to you?" he asked. "How did you get healed if not by the miraculous power of God?"

Still struggling with my worldview, I said, "Healing ceased after the Apostolic Age."

"No, Delores, the Bible doesn't teach that," he said. "Man says that not God. Can you show me in God's Word where he recalls the Holy Spirit or revokes the gifts of the Spirit?"

"No, I can't."

"No, because he never revoked them."

Then he asked me if I had any questions.

"Will I always know bad things about people?"

"No unless God is going to use you to set them free or help them through some issues they may be facing."

Ever so slowly my spiritual eyes began to open. I realized I wasn't going crazy; God had baptized me in the Holy Spirit.

Things looked a lot brighter as Velma and I drove back toward home. There were still some unanswered questions in my mind but God was putting the pieces of that giant jigsaw puzzle together one step at a time.

Sometime later the woman God revealed to me to be a lesbian came to visit me again. For some unknown reason she began telling me her story just as I had seen it in the Spirit.

As she related her story to me a strange thing happened. It was as though God was writing on my hand four things she had to do to be set free. They were so simple I was convinced they wouldn't work.

"There are four things I see you should do," I explained.

Then I shared them with her.

"Number one is you should truly repent and ask God to forgive you."

As soon as I completed the four things God asked her to do, I immediately forgot the last three and don't remember them to this day for they were only for her.

That day the woman got down on her knees in my living room and truly repented,

After she left Satan began kicking me all over the place. "You really made a fool out of yourself," he said to me. "How did you ever think you could help that woman? That's her life and you were meddling in it.

What do you think you're doing? You think you're so smart."

I felt terrible.

However, two months later the woman came to see me again.

She walked into our living room and the first thing she said was, "I'm free! I did it and God set me free!"

I was amazed. How could this be?

It was another miracle! Years later, she is still free and has no thought of her former sin. Her heart is filled with thanksgiving for Jesus set her free.

The Surrender

6

The last time we attended our Presbyterian church, the Lord moved on my heart and it was such a wonderful experience. Suddenly I saw those people in the church through the eyes of Jesus. For the first time I also loved them and had compassion on them. It brought me great pain and sorrow that they rejected me and never spoke openly of my healing. Yet that no longer bothered me. My heart held only love for them.

The first year after my healing was horrible! I fought Bill; he fought me. Bill insisted I accept the invitations I received to speak in churches. I insisted I stay home, plant flowers, and take care of my family, something I had been deprived of doing for nearly 20 years.

Hence there was a constant battle in our home that lasted for weeks even months.

Truthfully the problem was that I was in the driver's seat not God and nothing works very well when we get those positions reversed.

Following my healing Bill started spending long hours reading God's Word. Through the months he was saved, baptized in the Holy Spirit, and became much more spiritually perceptive that I was.

I even tried to tell God what to do. Can you imagine that?

When I would receive an invitation to speak in a

church I would say, "Alright God I'll go and tell what happened to me but don't heal anyone."

Things got pretty neat. A few days after I spoke in a church people would write me and say they were healed while I was speaking.

"Okay, God, I accept that," I would say. "You can do that."

That indicated I was totally filled with rebellion. Can you imagine me of all people telling God what he could and could not do – and how he could do it?

I received another call from Maggie with Kathryn's ministry. She said Kathryn wanted me to go to Oklahoma City to give my testimony during a meeting there.

I asked her to give me time to think about it.

Both Bill and Chris wanted me to go. Bill immediately knew why I had been invited but I was too dumb and naïve to understand.

Finally, I consented.

When we arrived at the auditorium in Oklahoma City where Kathryn was to minister, we met several people who had been in the service in Dallas the night I was healed.

The service began and there was singing and special music by Jimmy McDonald. Bill, Chris and I enjoyed the music.

Kathryn came onto the stat with her usual flair, grandly saying, "I believe in miracles."

She spoke for a while then abruptly turned to Jimmy McDonald and said, "Jimmy, a couple of weeks ago in Dallas we saw a woman healed and when it happened you cried."

"I want you to see that woman today," she added.

Then one of her assistants by the name of Donnie walked over toward me.

Suddenly I realized why she had invited me to the meeting.

There we were in a large packed auditorium and Kathryn was asking me to stand up in front of all those people and tell them what happened to me in Dallas.

Actually, I enjoyed the wonderful music and Jimmy McDonald's singing but I didn't want to speak to that crowd of people and they didn't scare me at all. I just wanted to be left alone so I could live my own life, adjust to my healing, and go about my business.

I grabbed Bill's arm. He took my hand and placed it back in my lap.

Bill was turning me loose and wasn't going to protect me and that was so disappointing.

Since I was in total rebellion the Lord worked through Bill.

When Donnie got to where we were sitting, I told him, "I'm not going."

Kathryn looked at me and said, "She doesn't want to have any part of me. She doesn't like me."

The audience broke into laughter.

Kathryn also laughed. She was laughing because she had seen so many others who had been healed act the same way I was acting.

Suddenly I said to myself, "Okay I'll show her."

I stood up and walked to the front of the auditorium and up onto the stage.

"Tell the people what happened to you," Kathryn ordered in her own inimitable persuasive way.

I told the people about my miraculous healing in Dallas.

After I concluded Kathryn ordered me to bend over.

I bent over and touched my toes even though I was wearing high-heeled shoes that night for the first time in years.

"Now, is everything alright?" Kathryn asked.

Once again rebellion rose up inside of me and I replied, "No, I still have a numb hand and there is burning around my back."

"Let's see what the Lord will do about that tonight," Kathryn said.,

When she touched me, I fell to the floor.

I'm not sure how long I laid there but when I woke up the numbness in my hand and burning in my back were completely gone never to return.

As we drove back to Arlington that night, I was torn up inside. I determined in my heart that I would never again speak before a crowd like that or go near Kathryn.

The next week I received another call from Maggie Hartner inviting me to go to California to make a video of my testimony with Kathryn.

"There's no way I'm going to do it," I told her. "I never want to be around that woman again."

When I started having muscle spasms in my back Bill told me I should go.

"No, I won't!" I yelled at him.

"Yes, you will go – you owe Kathryn that much."

"I don't owe her a thing."

"Yes, you do and you will go."

"I can't go and say, 'I'm healed,' when I'm having

muscle spasms in my back," I said trying to justify my rebellion.

Bill kept bugging me by saying, "You're going to get rid of those muscle spasms the very minute you decide to go to California."

Finally, I gave up and decided to go.

I wrote Maggie a letter and told her I would rather wait and go to California in November rather than October as Kathryn had wanted. I was trying to buy some extra time.

When I dropped the letter into the mailbox I breathed a prayer, "Lord, help them to forget all about me."

As soon as I mailed the letter the muscle spasms ceased just as Bill predicted.

I felt caught in a trap. Every time I tried to run away the trap would snap shut. It was a horrible feeling. It hadn't dawned on me that God was dealing with me through Kathryn. He had to use someone he could trust. That someone sure wasn't me.

God kept urging me to do things and I kept putting them off. Each afternoon when it was time for Bill to return home from work, I would get upset. I was convinced he could read my mind. He was always telling me things I should do, things that already were on my mind.

"I've got to get rid of this thought before Bill gets home." I would think to myself.

When Bill would arrive home, he would say, "You know, there's something I think you need to do."

I would cringe inside.

My husband was hearing things from the Lord and

being obedient to him.

I was not and it was a confused mixed-up period in our lives.

The time came for me to go to California.

Maggie told me that in addition to making the video with Kathryn, she wanted me to appear with her at a service in the Shrine Auditorium in Los Angeles.

For the first time in 20 years, I was alone on an airplane and after that alone in a hotel room. I felt pretty good. Bill wasn't there reading my mind and I could close the door and keep everyone out.

The next morning, several people from Kathryn's ministry came to take me to the CBS studio for the taping of the video. I suspected that meant sitting around listening to Kathryn staff talking about demons, evil spirits, deliverance, and healing – things I wasn't eager to hear about.

The taping went very well. Once again, I was able to share my healing testimony but I was greatly relieved when it was over.

The next morning one of Kathryn's aides called and asked me to go to the studio again.

"Why?" I asked.

"Because Kathryn wants you there."

"Well, who is Kathryn anyway?" I asked sarcastically.

The entire taping scenario chafed my old nature and brought out my rough edges.

Something very unusual happened after we finished the final taping. The CBS camera crew, the same crew that worked for the Sonny and Cher Show, came over and wanted to talk to me about my healing.

They asked me all kinds of questions.

"That's the first time this crew has ever wanted to talk to anyone on one of my programs," Kathryn later told me.

After the taping I decided to go to San Diego to see Winnie and Verne two of my best and longtime friends. I called Winnie the night before and told her I planned to visit them.

Only two months earlier they visited me in Arlington and saw me dying.

"Where are you? Are you in the hospital?" Winnie asked.

"No, I'm in Los Angeles."

"In the hospital?" she asked again.

"No, I'm coming to see you Winnie, I'll see you tomorrow."

Later Winnie told me that after she spoke with me, she told Verne, "Delores is in Los Angeles in a hospital. They have found some way to help her."

Winnie was expecting to see someone helping me down the steps from the airplane.

When she and Verne saw me walking by myself, Verne almost collapsed.

I walked into the passenger's lounge and saw him sitting in a chair chalk white and shaking like a leaf.

He kept saying, "Oh, my God! Oh, my God! What has happened?"

Of course, they had not heard about my healing but wanted to know all about it.

The visit with them was so very enjoyable but it was good to get back home to Bill and Chris.

Chris had changed so much in a short time after my

healing and I was thankful for him that I was healed and alive.

People continued to invite me to speak at various meetings. As usual and for some strange unknown reason, I told the Lord I didn't want people to be healed during the services. I told him I would appreciate it if he would heal them after the service was over and I could hear about it later.

Somehow Satan had convinced me that open manifestations of healings bordered on being a sideshow and I didn't want to picture myself as a sideshow faith healer.

But one night God said, "No more of this. No more."

People increasingly began being healed during the meetings and there was nothing I could do about it. But it took nearly two years before I could accept God's using me as a vessel of his healing power.

One night I was invited to minister to a group of people at Barksdale Air Force Base in Bossier City, Louisiana. During the service the Lord revealed to me that he was healing someone with a heart condition.

Out of obedience to God I invited that person to lift a hand and receive a healing.

No one moved but I knew for certain that a heart was being healed.

I saw a little boy standing on a chair with both of his hands in the air but I ignored him.

"I know a heart is being healed here tonight," I repeated.

The reason I was so certain a heart condition was being healed was because my own heart was behaving like the heart being healed. My heartbeat became irregular stopping and then starting again. As I continued asking someone to claim the healing of the heart, the little boy's mother placed her hand on his chest to check his heartbeat.

When my own heart became normal, I told the audience, "The heart is beating in a regular pattern now. Please claim it."

No one moved.

"Dear God, why doesn't someone accept it," I whispered.

But no one did.

After the service the little boy's mother brought him up to me. His name was Eric and his mother said he had been healed. She had placed her hand on his chest and felt his heart beating just as I had described it.

Then the mother told me a heartwarming story about her son. She explained that Eric was an orphan. No one would adopt him until he was a year old because of his heart condition. The workers at the adoption agency told prospective parents that Eric would have to have heart surgery when he was five years old. They also told them he would have only a 30 percent chance of survival.

Even though Eric had a bad heart, this woman and her husband adopted him as their own.

She also told me Eric was scheduled for open heart surgery the next week.

I looked at the little five-year-old boy and asked, "Do you want to thank Jesus for healing you?"

"Yes," he said.

I prayed a simple prayer asking God to put the assurance in Eric's heart that he truly had been healed.

After the prayer the little boy looked at me with his sparkling, chocolate-brown eyes and said, "Don't ever stop praying for people."

His words broke my heart.

Suddenly my own will, all my rebellion, and my desire to stay away from people vanished. That night, after little Eric said, "Don't ever stop praying (for people)," I surrendered to the Lord and told him I was willing to do whatever he wanted me to do and go wherever he wanted me to go and on his terms.

Oh, what a relief to be free of rebellion to let God be God. It was like the dawning of a bright new day in my life. It was the day for which God had patiently waited – the day my heart was broken and made right with him.

Sometime later we received a good report from Eric's mother. Doctors examined him and found nothing wrong with his heart. He never had the open-heart surgery. God healed him.

After I surrendered to the will of God a great change came over me. I felt so much better and happier.

Bill also felt better. He no longer had to endure my rebellion as he had all the long months since my healing.

We had become good friends with some of the people in the Methodist church in Bedford, Texas. They were charismatic Christians and loved us and welcomed us into their fellowship. I wanted to attend that church but God had other ideas.

He would reveal to Bill when I reached my coping limit at our Presbyterian church. That's when we would visit the Bedford church. Thank God he eventually revealed to Bill how long we should remain at our church.

The day after Kathryn Kuhlman died, we attended the morning service in our church. After the service, the pastor motioned for me to come over to where he was standing.

"I'm sorry to hear about Kathryn Kuhlman's death," he said.

I told him that Chris cried his heart out when he heard about it.

I told my pastor how I tried to comfort Chris by telling him, "She's in heaven now, Chris. I can just imagine her going in and saying, 'Oh, this is exactly the way I thought it would be. But that should be moved over here and this should be moved over there.' I can picture her rearranging heaven."

After hearing what I told Chris my pastor looked at me in silence for a minute then said, "That's not what I see."

"Oh?" I asked.

Suddenly it was apparent our conversation had become quite serious.

"I see her standing with the Lord and saying, 'Lord, there's one you used me to heal. There's Delores. Is she doing everything you would have her do?'"

His words stunned me.

"Well, Pastor, if I'm not, I'm sure I will be," I replied.

He nodded and that was the last conversation we ever had.

During Kathryn's illness God gave me a great love and compassion for her. He revealed to me what she was going through and I knew it wasn't easy for her.

She was perhaps one of the greatest women of our century one of God's chosen vessels. Had it not been for her I would have died a hopeless invalid never knowing the healing power of God.

When we left the church that day the lump in my stomach was gone and never returned. God kept us in that church all that time for my inner healing. Had I not learned to love those people and have compassion on them God never could have used me to serve him.

Of course, I still had visions of staying home, cooking, and taking care of my family but during that time something else kept flashing through my mind – visions of ministry. I initially shut the door not wanting to accept.

Bill knew what was happening. Until I surrendered God used him to keep me moving in the right direction.

I still had some rough times but things got much better. For instance, one day as I spoke to a group of believers, I saw Jesus. We were all sitting in a large circle. As I looked across the room Jesus was standing there. I knew it was Jesus for I could see him so clearly. He was holding a large loaf of bread in his outstretched hands and looking right at me

"Lord, I don't know what you're saying," I whispered plaintively.

Suddenly he turned toward me and I saw a deep hurt in his eyes and then I understood what he was saying: "I bring a whole loaf like this for each one of you and all you do is take a nibble. I have a whole loaf. Why aren't you taking it?"

The vision of Jesus and his probing question greatly

puzzled me.

Then God's Word spoke to from Philippians 4:19, *"But my God shall supply all your need according to His riches in glory by Christ Jesus."* (KJV)

Then I asked myself a question, "What do you think it is like in heaven? The angels praise him without ceasing."

I came to understand that the joy of heaven is ours right here but we have to reach out and take it and take the whole loaf, not just a few crumbs.

After seeing Jesus standing there before me holding the loaf of bread, I knew I had to take it all in order to be all he wanted me to be.

So, I did.

As I followed the leading of the Lord into a full-time ministry of salvation and healing there were stills some doubts in my mind. But God was gracious and patient and answered all my questions and overcame all my doubts.

While living in Arlington Bill and I formed the Fellowship Foundation, Inc. The organization would serve as the physical arm of our spiritual ministry.

However, for some time both Bill and I felt the inner urging to move to Shreveport, Louisiana, where we were to make our home. God had established a strong group of supporters there who pledged to assist us in our ministry.

Leaving Arlington was no easy decision. Our son Doug and his wife Ann and our grandchildren lived nearby and our move would take us far away from them. Also, Chris now 17 had lived in Arlington most of his life and would have to leave his roots – the only city and home he had ever known. And Bill would have to resign his good job and take another at half the pay.

Also, there was the question of age. Both of us felt we were too old to begin a full-time ministry.

But we decided if we were to receive the full loaf of bread Jesus held out to us in the vision, we would have to do everything he wanted – not what we wanted.

We were convinced it was his will for us to move so we stepped out in faith, determined to live one day at a time. We knew that God would take care of all our needs. Has he not promised: *"Lo, I am with you always; even unto the end of the world..."* (Matt. 28:20) (KJV)

So, we accepted God's loving invitation to move to Shreveport.

We placed the days and years of ministry squarely in his hands for it was his ministry and we were blessed to be a part of it.

7
The Ministry

Although I didn't realize it on that unforgettable night when Jesus healed me, he also baptized me in the Holy Spirit and bestowed on me the gift of healing as explained by the Apostle Paul in the twelfth chapter of the book of First Corinthians.

Through the months the Lord taught Bill and me the meaning of that baptism. Until we receive it and are filled, we cannot consistently manifest the fruit of the Spirit.

God wants to wash us until we are thoroughly clean. Without that baptism it is difficult to have the full joy of the Lord. That is the reason so many Christians are sad as they sit in church worship services on Sunday not even knowing why.

You can always know when you are with Spirit-filled Christians because there is so much joy among them. There is a light in their eyes that never goes out for they have the fullness of the Spirit within them.

It was necessary for me to receive that baptism when I was healed for I didn't know how to love people. Oh, I could sort of love those in my family and maybe someone who was having a hard time and needed help.

But I couldn't go to someone, put my arms around them, and say, "I love you."

Since love is the basic fruit of the Spirit, God could not fully use me until I showed the love of Jesus to other people.

People ask me today, "Why do I need the baptism in the Holy Spirit?"

"Because Jesus commanded us to receive it. Without it we are not whole. It brings boldness for witnessing into our lives and healing for us. When our spirits are healed, it often results in physical healing," I explain.

Bill and I were no strangers to the ministry just new to physical healing.

During our long months of preparation God already had performed some miraculous healings.

I remember the first time ever I dealt with a terminal patient.

Janice, a pastor's wife, asked me if I would go with her to Houston, Texas to pray for her friend Sandy who was 26 years old and dying of cancer. Surgeons in West Texas where she lived had removed one breast and performed a colostomy that allowed her bowels to move through a tube into a plastic bag attached to her side.

Samples taken from her glands revealed she was eaten up with cancer. Her surgeons recommended she go to M. D. Anderson Hospital in Houston to see if there was anything that could be done for her.

After she arrived there, radiologists discovered the cancer had spread throughout her body.

Janice and I drove to Houston and planned to rent a room for the night and go to the hospital the next morning to pray for Sandy. However, when we arrived it was apparent that Satan wanted to keep us from

It's Time To Be Healed

praying for her.

There were so many conventions in the city that all the hotels and motels were full and, since Janice was pregnant and due to have her baby at any time, we had to find a place to spend the night.

We thought that perhaps we should return home, but suddenly – in the Spirit – I knew we dare not go home.

Janice had an aunt and uncle that lived near Houston so we thought we might stay with them. She called them four times but there was no answer.

By 10:30 p.m. we were getting a little desperate.

Finally, I said to Janice, "We're staying in Houston even if we have to sleep in the car and even if you have your baby in the car, God will take care of us."

She agreed.

She called her aunt and uncle again and they were home and invited us to spend the night with them.

The next morning, we went to the hospital so see Sandy.

When we arrived and went to her room a nurse informed us Sandy had been taken downstairs for some tests and probably would be gone most of the day.

So, we went to the waiting room where we met her dear mother who was there supporting her daughter.

We greeted her warmly.

"They've taken her downstairs," she said. "You just missed her."

"That's alright," I said. "We're going to pray."

We prayed and asked God to perform a miracle and bring Sandy back to her hospital room.

Then we waited.

In just a few minutes the elevator door opened and two orderlies wheeled her back into her room.

She told us that for some unknown reason she asked the doctors if she could return to her room for one hour even though she did not know we were there to visit her.

I took one look at her weakened condition and thought, "God, I'm not talking to this girl about healing unless you show me exactly what I should say for she's too close to death."

Janice brought three books to give to Sandy. Among them was *The Miracles* by Dr. Richard Casdorph which included a chapter on my miraculous healing.

She placed the books on a table beside Sandy's bed.

Sandy reached over, picked up the books, and began thumbing through them.

"*The Miracles*, what's it about?" she asked.,

"It's about people who were healed," Janice replied.

"Oh," she said and laid the book down.

A few minutes later Sandy again picked up the miracles book, opened it and said, "Delores Winder – that's you? Were you healed?"

"Yes," I replied.

Then I silently prayed, "Okay, Lord, I'll talk to her about healing."

So, I told Sandy what God had done for me.

"You mean you were dying and you were healed?"

"Yes."

"That's really something."

"Do you believe it?"

"Yes, I do."

We prayed for her healing.

By the time we finished praying for her the orderlies returned with a gurney to take her back downstairs to continue the tests.

As she was leaving the room she looked back at Janice and me and said, "Don't leave."

Both Janice and I noticed that her face looked completely different than before.

The doctors kept her only a short time and the orderlies brought her back to her room and put her in bed.

As soon as the orderlies left the room, Sandy got out of bed and said, "I'm going to take a shower."

A nurse looked in the room and saw her getting out of bed.

"You must stay in bed," the nurse ordered

"No, I'm going to take a shower," Sandy replied and then she began singing as she washed her hair.

The nurse summoned two orderlies to help get her back in bed but when they heard her singing in the shower they left the room.

"I feel great," she said as she came out of the shower a towel wrapped around her head.

Then she sat down on her bed.

Later that afternoon the doctors said they wanted to give her a report on the tests they had run after we prayed for her.

Before she left the room once again, she said, "Don't leave I need to have you here until we hear what the doctors have to say."

Once again, she met with a battery of 12 doctors who were working on her case.

They were amazed and gave her the miraculous

results.

One doctor came to where we were waiting and asked, "Did you hear that they couldn't find any trace of the cancer?"

No," I answered smiling.

When they brought Sandy back to her room she looked like a new woman.

It was a time of great rejoicing in the Lord.

However, one of the doctors suggested she should go ahead and have chemotherapy.

I looked at Sandy and said, "Ask God to close the door if he doesn't want you to have it."

She told the doctors she wanted to leave the hospital and go to the apartment to be with her husband and mother.

The doctors consented but asked her to return to the hospital in a few days for the chemotherapy treatment.

When she returned to the hospital for the chemotherapy the Lord closed the door through her own doctor.

"Sandy, I think we'll wait a week to start the treatment," he said.

Sandy continually prayed about whether she should have the treatments.

When she returned to the hospital her doctor took one look at her and said, "I don't want to do anything today. Why don't you go home for three weeks then we'll see how you are doing."

Several weeks later, Sandy came to our home in Shreveport and rang the doorbell. When I opened the door, I didn't recognize her.

"You don't know who I am, do you?" she asked.

"No, I don't," I replied.

"I'm Sandy," she said, a broad smile on her face.

What a blessing it was to witness the goodness of God in healing her! It sent sensations of joy all through my body and praised welled up in my heart.

People often ask me the question: Why are people so fearful of cancer?

I believe cancer is a tool of the devil and even the word cancer frightens people.

Doctors build on that fear when they say, "Oh, it's cancer – there's nothing we can do."

God revealed to me that as far as his healing power is concerned cancer is nothing more than a common cold.

However, most people react to the disease with great fear and that is a hindrance to their healing.

During those early days the Lord kept speaking to me, saying, "Educate my people and keep the balance."

That is everything! A good balance is the first priority in preaching the Gospel. Unfortunately, among Spirit-baptized believers today there is not a strong emphasis on winning lost people to the Lord. A lot of people get all excited and want to see miracles. But they soon forget that Jesus' first priority is to bring people into the Kingdom – not miracles, healing, or deliverance.

During all of our healing services Bill and I emphasize that people must be saved. What good will healing be for them if they die and go to hell?

It amazes me how many church members are not saved. We meet and deal with them all the time. We should never take a person's salvation for granted just because his/her name is on the church membership roll.

Churches have become so socially oriented that many who join them are totally oblivious to the need to commit their lives to Jesus Christ.

Remember that the word *salvation* relates to the whole person – body, soul, and spirit. It means salvation from sin and death but it also includes healing and deliverance. Jesus came to minister to the whole person and we must follow that example.

As the news of my testimony spread God opened doors for me to receive invitations from all over the country to minister his healing power.

During a women's meeting in Sarasota, Florida, some of her friends brought a crippled woman to the service. She was so severely crippled, her friends had to carry her into the meeting place.

When I saw them bring her in I became a little irritated. Sometimes well-meaning people drag sick people into meetings when those people had rather not be there.

But did God teach me something that day!

The crippled woman was in such a sad condition that some people might think the Lord could not heal her. She was so debilitated the people sitting next to her had to hold her up in her chair to keep her from falling.

I prayed and asked the Lord to let me forget she was there since my attention was all wrapped up in her sad condition rather than ministering the Word to all the people.

After my teaching was completed, the ladies brought

the helpless woman to the altar.

I laid hands on her and prayed for her and she was slain in the Spirit.

Then I continued praying for the other ladies who had come to the altar for the prayer of faith.

Four months later, I began receiving reports and the name about a woman who had been healed in the Sarasota women's meeting but I didn't remember her name.

Two years later I met the woman at a Bible conference in Florida.

She came running up to me and asked, "Delores, do you know who I am?"

"No, I don't think so."

"I'm Mary!"

"That's good it's nice to know you."

"No, you don't understand, I'm the crippled woman who was healed in Sarasota!"

Together we rejoiced in the Lord!

One evening while ministering the Word at a Full Gospel Businessmen's meeting in Hope, Arkansas, a woman whose eyes were clouded with cataracts came to the altar for prayer. When I first saw her clouded eyes, I really didn't have the faith to believe she would be healed.

I laid hands on her and offered a simple supplication to the Lord for the cataracts to be taken away. Then I moved among the others standing at the altar and one by one prayed for them.

A few minutes later someone took my arm, pointed toward the lady who had the cataracts, and said, "Come and look at her eyes."

We watched as the cataracts melted away from her eyes.

I looked and saw color in her eyes. Before, there was only a cloudy film.

Her eyes continued healing during the evening and when we went to her church the next morning her eyes were completely clear.

Praise be to God!

The wonderful people of the Lady of Fatima Catholic Church of Monroe, Louisiana, often invited Bill and me to minister. God had poured out his Spirit on those people and they had experienced a number of miracles of healing.

During one of our meetings a woman with a large growth on her neck came for prayer. As I looked at the growth, I could see it was about the size of a hen egg.

We laid hands on the woman and as we prayed, we saw the growth begin to decrease in size little by little until it was completely gone.

There was great rejoicing among those charismatic Catholics as they witnessed another manifestation of the healing power of God.

God also had a lot of teaching to do in my life and at times I was a slow learner. For instance, it took some doing for me to accept people being slain in the Spirit.

Sometime after my healing – when I was slain in the Spirit two times – I began to feel strange sensations in my hands like electric currents going through them. It frightened me for I sensed it was the power of God flowing through me.

For days I kept my hands in my pockets not wanting to touch anyone fearing something strange might happen.

One day while teaching a Bible lesson to a group of women in Arlington I took and elderly woman by the hand and see fell out in the Spirit. I reached down to help her, touched another woman, and she fell out. Then I brushed against two other ladies and they went down under the power of the Holy Spirit.

Frightened, I started to run out of the meeting place, bumped into a woman a wheelchair and she fell under the Spirit. Another woman backed into me and she went down.

I grabbed my keys and pocketbook and ran to my car. I immediately went to a Spirit-filled pastor whom I loved and trusted to ask him what had happened.

"What were you doing when it happened," he asked.

"Trying to get away."

Very carefully he explained the purpose of God in taking people out under the power of the Spirit. He said God does it when he wants to minister to a person's spirit to provide spiritual help for them.

He also walked me through various Scriptures that shed light on the question.

He explained that during a post-resurrection appearance of Jesus, the phenomenon occurred when the keepers of the sepulcher saw the angel his raiment white as snow.

"The Word says: *'And for fear of him the keepers did shake, and became as dead men'*" (Matt. 28:4 KJV).

Also, the pastor explained John 18:3-6 to me.

"The passage begins with Judas bringing the officers and chief priests to the Garden of Gethsemane to arrest Jesus. The men were carrying lanterns, torches, and weapons.

"When Jesus asked them, *'Whom seek ye?'* they answered, *'Jesus of Nazareth'* (John 18:6 KJV).

"The Word also says: *'As soon then as He had said unto them, I am He, they went backward and fell to the ground'"* (John 18:6 KJV).

The pastor also explained that on another occasion a father brought to Jesus his son who had a dumb spirit. When Jesus ministered deliverance to the boy, Mark 9:26 says: *"And the spirit cried, and rent him sore, and came out of him: and he was as one dead; insomuch that many said, He is dead"* (KJV).

The pastor told me about how when the silver-haired apostle John saw the vision on the Isle of Patmos, he *"...fell at His feet as dead..."* as noted in Revelation 1:17 (KJV).

He suggested that I try to find out what God had done for those women who were slain in the Spirit during the meeting in Arlington that day.

So, I contacted several of them and asked them what God had done for them while they were out under the power of the Spirit.

One lady told me she had not wept in 12 years yet when she came out from under the power, she wept freely.

Another lady said she had never before felt the love of God. When slain in the Spirit that day she said she felt cushioned in the arms of Jesus and heard him telling her he loved her.

Another lady said she received a healing and another received the baptism in the Holy Spirit.

After speaking with that pastor, I better understood

what God had done that day.

I humbly admit that at times there still were doubts in my mind about it until one day I heard the voice of God saying to me, "You take care of your business and I'll take care of this."

Now I leave it completely in his hands.

Parenthetically, praise God for that Spirit--filled pastor! He helped me so much that day. All my fears of that supernatural phenomenon vanished and never returned.

The Great Physician

8

One evening while ministering in a Presbyterian church in Shreveport the Spirit-filled pastor made a quite unusual prayer request. He said one of his friends, a prominent Shreveport attorney, had gone to St. Luke's hospital in Houston for cardiovascular surgery. The minister volunteered to stand in proxy for the attorney as I prayed for him.

Everyone in the service felt the power and presence of God as we laid hands on the minister.

That night the Lord gave us the assurance that the attorney was healed.

Later the attorney related the following story to us:

"Some weeks before all the people began to pray for me, I sensed numbness in my right thigh and I immediately went to see an orthopedic surgeon who was unable to find a pulse in my thigh or ankle. The doctor concluded that the blood supply in my right leg had become blocked and suggested that I immediately be hospitalized.

"While I was in the hospital the doctor called in several specialists including a reputable cardiovascular surgeon to confirm his findings. None of the specialists could find a pulse in my thigh. The consensus among four physicians was that I must have surgery.

"Arrangements were made with Dr. Denton Cooley,

the far-famed Houston heart surgeon to perform the operation at St. Luke's Hospital.

"Meanwhile, hundreds of people were called to prayer for me including those at the Presbyterian church who laid hands on the man in proxy for me.

"I checked into St. Luke's and underwent extensive tests. A few days later, just before the surgery, a young resident entered my room.

"'Do you mind if I see if I can find a pulse in your leg?'" the resident asked.

"Of course," I replied.

"After briefly examining the leg the young resident said, "'I'm not so sure about your vascular problem but that's not my job.'

"Dr. Cooley, accompanied by six other doctors, visited my room for a pre-operation examination. After carefully examining me, he concluded that I did not need surgery. But he suggested that a neurologist conduct another examination just for confirmation.

"The neurologist gave me a thorough examination and agreed with Dr. Cooley that surgery was not necessary.

"I really praised the Lord for I knew the Great Physician had healed me!

"When I returned home, I went back to my own doctor and told him the story of what had happened. He checked me again and found a strong pulse in my leg.

"How could I have missed the pulse?" the doctor asked. "I would take an oath that is wasn't there before."

"'You didn't miss it,'" I told him." "'I've had hundreds, maybe thousands of people praying for me. God made this old body and he knew how to repair it.'"

One evening while ministering at the same Presbyterian church in Shreveport I noticed a Catholic nun in the audience. The church was filled with people seeking healing from their afflictions but I kept noticing the Catholic sister who probably was in her early sixties.

I felt impressed of the Lord to invite her to the altar to minister with me.

She agreed.

There was a woman standing at the altar for prayer who had a large growth on her face.

"Do you want to minister healing to this woman?" I asked the sister.

"I don't know how; I've never done this before," the sister whispered to me.

"Would you like to pray for her?"

"Yes, I'll try."

"No, you'll not try. You do your part and God will do the rest."

"Alright."

She laid hands on the growth on the woman's face and prayed. When she took her hand away the growth was gone. The first time the dear Catholic sister prayed for someone to be healed God performed a great miracle through her!

This is such a great day for the church for God is pouring out his Spirit on all flesh!

I believe the day is at hand when we will see more and more churches – both Protestant and Catholic – carrying out the full ministry of Jesus. When this takes place there will no longer be any need for a ministry such as mine for the healing ministry will have returned to the church where it belongs. Our Lord's perfect will for pastors is for them to stand strong in the pulpits throughout this nation to proclaim the Full Gospel.

During my long years of illness not one pastor ever prayed for me to be healed. They did pray that I would be able to endure all the suffering and pain.

And did I ever endure it!

But that is not the prayer Jesus taught us. He said he would heal us and deliver us. When we know what God has available for us, we can come to him and ask for it. Then we start appropriating what he has promised. We say, "Lord, although I still have pain in my body, I believe that you are healing me because your Word says you will heal me."

Our physical body begins to change as our minds, bodies, and spirits come into one accord with God's Word. The best way for us to be healed is to be in accord with his Word for it is basically through his Word that we hear from him.

All Spirit-baptized believers can hear God's call to minister. The gifts of the Spirit can operate in a downtown office building just as in a healing and miracle service. But most people have never caught on to that truth. Those gifts should be in operation wherever we are and whatever we are doing in our daily lives.

Bill and I are just two people but the Lord has graciously allowed our ministry to touch thousands.

I see the thousands, yea millions of Spirit-baptized believers who work in downtown office buildings, factories, hospitals, and government offices. If they would catch the vision of ministry where they work it would be a bright new day for the Kingdom of God.

Homemakers can also minister. Be sure to teach your children about Jesus and minister to them. They receive so quickly.

Once when Bill and I were guests in the home of some friends their little girl by the name of Kimmy jumped up in my lap and said, "Delores, my nose is stopped up and I can't breathe very good and can't sleep. Would you pray for me?"

Her parents were talking long distance on the telephone as I prayed, "Jesus, you know that Kimmy has to get some sleep. I'm just going to ask you to open up her nose and clear her sinuses so she can sleep."

"Thank you," Kimmy said. "Whew, thank you," she added and went to bed and to a deep sleep.

Children readily receive but mothers and fathers often don't bother to pray for them when they are sick yet some of those mothers and fathers may be considered very spiritual people. They often are out ministering to others while neglecting the ministry to their own children in the home. It only takes a minute to allow the love of Jesus and his healing power to touch a child.

People who have witnessed great miracles and the healing power of God should stay excited about what God can do for the healing of their children.

Sometimes all we have is the name of Jesus. I've known mothers that would sit by the beds of sick children and just repeat the name of Jesus and they would see their children being healed.

One year Bill and I ministered in Massachusetts, New Hampshire, and Ohio where in our meetings God performed many wonderful miracles.

In a meeting in Ohio a man with a tumor on his spine came to the altar for prayer. X-rays clearly revealed the tumor and his surgeons told him it had to be removed.

We prayed a simple prayer for his healing and God touched him.

When he went to the hospital for surgery the surgeon decided to X-ray his spine again before the operation. The result startled him for the tumor was gone.

The man rejoiced in the healing power of our wonderful Lord!

Also, in Ohio a woman who had been confined to a wheelchair for three years came to our service.

During the service the Lord spoke to me and said someone in the audience could rise up and walk.

Although the Lord did not reveal to me who it was, he did reveal it to Bill who went to the woman in the wheelchair and said, "You can get up now."

She stood up and walked around praising the Lord.

God also healed a Florida woman of multiple sclerosis.

When she came into our meeting, she was in such bad condition that the toes on one of her feet were doubled under.

We prayed for her.

Then I said, "Come on, let's walk."

She stood up but sat back down.

"My toes are cramping," she said.

We removed her shoes and watched as her toes began to unfold. They continued straightening until she was totally healed.

Before her healing we had sensed blackness around her. Now she is a radiant Christian through whom the love of the Lord shines brightly.

Oh, the wonders of our Lord! How he wants to heal his people. He already has provided everything needed for that healing. All we must do is receive it. Every day he proves that he is the Great Physician.

Inner Healing

9

God's Word has a lot to say about inner healing. Jesus said he came to earth to heal the brokenhearted – that's inner healing.

The Book of Proverbs is filled with good advice on how we can stay well inwardly and spiritually.

There are going to be times in our lives when we feel anger, resentment, frustration, and unforgiveness. But these only linger if we fail to lay them at the foot of the cross. We are the ones who suffer if we allow such dangerous emotions to hang around.

During these years of ministry, I've met many people who carry unforgiveness in their hearts. It is the most devastating of all inner emotions.

If you the reader cannot control your emotions you must pray something like this, "Lord, I lay my awful emotions down and through you I forgive that person who has done me wrong. Even if I can't do it by myself right now, I'm going to forgive that person because you forgave them. Now I'm asking you to give me the kind of feelings I should have in my heart."

This is the cleaning process of our emotions and inner healing.

Medical science acknowledges that much physical sickness comes from spiritual sickness. For instance, when you tell a lie certain glandular secretions attack your stomach and can over a period of time make you sick.

One day the Lord showed me we have valleys inside us. When all our resentment, hatred, bitterness, and other harmful emotions settle into those valleys we often think, "This will pass and I'll forget it."

That's a dangerous assumption. When we forget something, it only means the issue has been exiled to our subconscious. Hidden away a little scab forms over our memories and seals them but it will continue festering there.

Jesus wants to peel that scab away, clean out our valleys, and allow the Holy Spirit to fill us with good things.

Essentially, psychiatry seeks to accomplish through physical means what God does through spiritual means.

The late Senator Talbot Fields of Arkansas was in a lot of trouble with the law. He was on trial and facing a long prison sentence.

A friend told him about our ministry and one day during the trial he called me from Arkansas.

After introducing himself and telling me a little about his problems, he said, "I want you to pray for me. I'm in trouble and it looks like I'm going to jail – everything is lost."

As we began to pray, suddenly I saw the Lord breaking him free and the Lord also showed the senator he would not go to prison.

We had a real hallelujah time right there on the telephone.

When the judge later dismissed the charges against

It's Time To Be Healed

him, Senator Fields raised his hands in the courtroom and praised God saying that it was by his power that he was a free man.

Sometime later I received a letter from the senator's wife. She reminded me that when I had prayed for him on the telephone, he received an inner healing and he was set free from the chains that had bound his spirit.

She did not elaborate nor did I inquire as to the nature of the inner healing. That was between the senator and God.

Senator Fields since has passed away but during his last years here on earth he proved to be a remarkable man. After he was healed inwardly, God provided a way out of his legal entanglements apparently assured he would straighten up his life.

The senator became the founder and president of the Full Gospel Businessmen's chapter in Hope, Arkansas, and once invited me to minister in one of their meetings.

During the waning days of his life, he praised the Lord and never failed to testify that it was God who set him free – inside and outside.

There was a woman in her 70s that attended one of our meetings in Florida. Crippled with arthritis, during the invitation she came to the altar for prayer.

I don't believe in blanket prayers such as, "God, heal them." When I face someone in need, I pray that God will reveal their need to me.

Often, I don't even hear what a person is saying when they come for prayer. Their request may not represent their real need but may be the result of the real need.

In the case of the woman that came for healing of arthritis the Lord spoke the word *forgiveness* to me.

"Is there someone you should forgive or ask forgiveness of?" I asked her.

"No," she said with a sweet expression on her face.

I wanted to believe her for she appeared to be an honest sincere person.

But once again the Lord said, "No, *unforgiveness.*"

"Are you sure there isn't someone you need to forgive or ask forgiveness of?" I asked her again.

"No," she answered, a puzzled look on her face.

"It just can't be," I thought for she appears confused at my questions.

As I began to pray for her, the Lord spoke to me a third time: "I said *unforgiveness.* Don't pray a general prayer."

I stopped praying and said, "I'm sorry but the Lord is showing me there is unforgiveness in your life."

Tears rolled down her cheeks and I felt as though I was badgering her. Yet the Lord had spoken and I had to stand on what he said.

Then the Lord spoke the word *brother.*

"What about your brother?" I asked.

Her look could have burned holes through me.

"You do have a brother?"

"Yes."

"Do you have a problem with him?"

"No, I have had nothing to do with him for a long time."

I was shocked.

"What do you mean you haven't had anything to do with him?"

It's Time To Be Healed

"I just don't."

"Because you had a problem?"

"Yes, but it doesn't bother me."

"Look at your hands, your legs, your feet. So, you want to get rid of this arthritis? Then you are going to have to forgive your brother or ask his forgiveness."

She glared at me.

"Do you want to be free from your arthritis?"

"Yes."

For a moment she had some questions in her mind as to whether she wanted to pay such a price to be healed for she wasn't sure the price was worth it.

"Are you willing to forgive him? Will you ask him to forgive you?"

"Yes."

"How long have you had this arthritis?"

"About 12 years."

Then it hit her like a bomb. Suddenly she realized what she had just said.

"You're going to forgive him because the Lord spoke it."

"Yes."

After I prayed with her, I said, "Now you are going to have to either write or call your brother and talk to him about this. Tell him how you have forgiven him and ask him to forgive you."

"No, I don't have to write him a letter."

"Yes, you do."

"No, I won't need to call him or write him – he only lives two doors away from me."

As soon as she forgave her brother the arthritis went away.

Only two doors away yet they have been filled with bitterness toward each other for 12 years! And that bitterness caused her to be crippled with arthritis.

Sometime later a friend who knew the situation between the woman and her brother explained the problem to me.

She told me that the fight between them was over a mere $3,000 that each of them thought they should have received when their mother died.

"That woman is so rich she could buy or sell half of this city," the friend said.

What a tragedy for a wealthy woman to suffer from arthritis because she felt her brother had cheated her out of $3,000.

Let me give you a word of caution about inner healing. After you receive it, Satan will try to bring the problem back. Even though you are free of it the evil one will whisper the thought of it in your ear.

At that point you must take authority and say, "No, Satan. Praise God I'm free of it because of Jesus."

There are also times when God gives inner healing through weeping. Some people just cry it out.

A friend of mine wept for six weeks after he was saved. It took that long for the Holy Spirit to clean out all the guilt that had built up in him through the years. After six weeks of weeping, he was set free.

The beautiful thing is that God knows how uniquely he made each of us and he deals with us in different ways. That's why I don't like blanket prayers. I want to hear from God as I minister. Only then will I know through the person's uniqueness how God wants to deal with them.

There was another woman who received a miraculous inner healing. Her problem was fear. It constantly ripped her apart and caused emotional and even mental problems.

For years she had lived in a state of depression. She had electric shock and other treatments but nothing helped.

When we prayed for her the Lord set her free. Now she is such a joy to the Lord and her friends. She is bubbly all the time. She works in a large office building and the Lord has given her a ministry of healing there.

She says a coworker will say to her, "I have a headache, will you go to the rest room and pray for me?"

The two will go to the rest room for the prayer of faith for healing.

She often prays for the sick in the rest room and invariably they are healed and she rejoices in that ministry.

Not once has she ever said, "Oh, I think God is going to take me away from here and place me in a full-time ministry." She knows she is where God wants her and she can minister to people and witness to the Lord right where she is.

Even men in her office come to her for prayer.

I probably will never work in a downtown office building but God needs ministers there eight hours a day and 40 hours a week. What a revelation it would be for people to realize the gifts of God are for all Christians to be ministered everywhere.

A friend told me a beautiful story of his wife's inner healing of bad memories. She carried bitterness in her heart toward a friend and it bothered her so that she couldn't sleep.

One evening she prayed that the Lord would forgive her and help her forget her bitterness toward her friend. The next morning when she awakened, she remembered praying for the healing of her memory but she could no longer remember the one against whom she had held the bitterness.

Unforgiveness is such a destructive emotion. When sin grips us, it can cause our whole world to become topsy-turvy. Jesus, you recall had quite a lot to say about the subject.

Let me share with you a little exercise I've learned about dealing with unforgiveness.

Just pray, "Lord, I want to lay it down. I'm going to forgive that person through Jesus. If I can't do it by myself right now, I'll forgive because Jesus paid the price for it. I'll forgive through you. And I'm asking you to give the kind of feelings in my heart that I should have."

God promises us in his Word that after our sins are forgiven, he remembers them no more. He completely forgets them and his attitude toward those sins is that they never existed.

There are times when we have trouble forgiving and forgetting our own sins. If God does not remember our sins, who is it that reminds us of them? The devil of course. Often it requires inner healing to be able to forgive ourselves and forget past sins.

A friend of mine spent several years in prison but now is saved and a powerful witness for Jesus.

Some time ago one of his acquaintances asked him,

"What were you in prison for?"

"Listen, God has forgotten all about that and I'm not going to give the devil a chance to bring it back up. It's covered by the blood of Jesus," my friend replied.

That's right! God forgave and forgot his sins. Why shouldn't he?

Inner healing deals with deep-seated emotions buried deep within us that often go awry. Hurts, fears, resentment, anger, unforgiveness, doubt, bitterness, bad memories, phobias, and lot of other problems need the touch of the hand of God to set us free.

When we carry these harmful emotions too long, we sometimes invite demons and unclean spirits into our lives. Demonic oppression can cause a Christian to be as miserable as one who is possessed. In our meetings, it is almost always the Christian, and not the unbeliever, who wants to be set free from those harmful emotions.

You recall that Jesus called an unclean spirit out of a man in the synagogue. Since the man was in the synagogue he must have been worshipping God.

Inner healing takes place through a supernatural act of God. There is nothing hokey-pokey about it. What appears supernatural to us is natural with God. We must allow it to be the same with us as we walk in the Spirit.

There are times when God gives me a picture as I minister healing of memories.

One day as I ministered to a woman experiencing deep emotional distress, she said she had no idea why she was suffering emotionally. But as we discussed her issue, she mentioned that her father was an alcoholic.

Suddenly in the Spirit I saw the picture of a four-year-old child sitting in the middle of a bed screaming. She had her arms over her face as though trying to hide.

"Stop!" she shouted as I described the scene to her.

"What happened in that room?" I asked.

Then she remembered why she was screaming: her father was beating her mother. She held her hands over her eyes to keep from seeing the cruel incident. That memory was buried so deep in her subconscious that it created emotional distress and depression.

As I prayed for her, she saw that Jesus was with her holding her in his arms and protecting her. She also realized that he could heal her of her emotional suffering and he did.

Praise God!

Later she told me she always harbored bad feelings toward her father but had never understood why. She also confessed she had become a heavy drinker like her father.

After God set her free, she knew the next step was to go to her father to help set him free.

When she shared with him what God had done in her life it had an amazing impact on him. He received her testimony and it led to his conversion to Christ and rapid spiritual growth.

She was set free from the painful, destructive emotional illness and both she and her father from drinking. It all occurred because the Lord dug up an emotional trauma that had plagued her from childhood.

There are times when emotional suffering deteriorates into mental illness. The mind then becomes tormented by runaway emotions.

This can be caused by a number of circumstances: disappointments, bad childhood memories, and too many demands by parents.

Often, psychiatrists (particularly Spirit-filled ones) can help these people.

But remember, God is the Master Psychiatrist. He created the psyche in each of us and knows better than anyone how to heal it.

The Holy Spirit can walk a person back to the time and place where the initial seeds of mental illness were sown because he was right there with you at that time. The person may not have been aware of his presence, but he was there.

Disobedience is a major cause of illness. The Apostle Paul emphasized the relationship of sickness to disobedience when he wrote a letter to the Christians in the city of Corinth:

"Therefore, whoever eats the bread and drinks the cup of the Lord in an unworthy manner will be guilty of sinning against the body and blood of the Lord. A man ought to examine himself before he eats of the bread and drinks of the cup. For anyone who eats and drinks without recognizing the body of the Lord eats and drinks judgment on himself. That is why many among you are weak and sick, and a number of you have fallen asleep" (1 Cor. 11:27-30).

Unworthy simply means unconfessed sin in a person's life. Thus, disobedience to God when allowed to continue unconfessed can lead to sickness which can lead to death even among Christians.

There are some ministers who have hangups about

women preachers particularly charismatic women preachers. They may require inner healing of attitudes toward women God has called into the ministry.

A young pastor of one of the largest churches in a metropolitan city came to our service. He held a doctor of theology degree and was just a typical, proud young man, handsome, brilliant, and at the apex of success. Also, he was being groomed for a high position of leadership in his denomination.

He knew the Word, at least the printed Word, and was a gifted, anointed preacher. His preaching brought people to salvation in tears. He faithfully preached the Word and did not resort to emotional chicanery.

But this pastor had a problem – his little girl was sick with a dread disease. Suddenly he faced a problem for which he had no answer. His inability to deal with the illness dealt a severe blow to his pride, haughtiness, and arrogance.

As his daughter's condition worsened, God began to give him a glimpse of something new in his experience.

One day he opened the newspaper and saw my picture with an advertisement stating I would be ministering in a Presbyterian church in his city.

Later, he told me that when he saw my picture the Lord spoke to him but he didn't understand what it meant.

He also said that every time he saw my picture in the paper, he was drawn by some inner urging to attend one of our meetings. He laughed at the idea.

One day he drove to the grocery store to pick up a loaf of bread for his wife. On the way he turned on the car radio and picked up my broadcast.

He turned off the program.,

Then he had a change of heart. "I'm going to listen to her and see if I understand anything she says."

When he arrived at the store, he waited in the car until the program was over.

He returned home not realizing what was happening to him for he had a strong feeling that he should call me.

Hence, he called our office and told our secretary he wanted to see me.

But I was out of town.

It really wasn't the time for us to talk – he wasn't ready.

He told me that during the next seven months every time he turned on the radio, he picked up my radio program.

One day a layman in his church went to him and suggested he take his daughter to one of our meetings. He and his wife brought their daughter to our meeting the next night,

Earlier we received a call from him telling us they would be attending our meeting.

I suggested that I pray for his daughter before the service began.

One of the things the Lord taught me is to be careful with people, particularly ministers, not to put them on display or in a precarious position.

Prior to the service I prayed for the little girl so there was no spectacle made of her well-known father.

The minister and his wife remained for the service. During the invitation he came to the altar and stood there in prayer. That night the Lord broke a proud man.

Then he and his wife brought their precious little girl to the altar.

His beautiful wife was a timid person and I could only imagine what it cost her to come to the altar that night.

After the service he said, "I need to talk to you."

We set up an appointment and a few days later I shared with him the wonderful things God was doing.

He received everything I told him and said, "I know this is of the Lord."

As God continued to break him, his little daughter became worse. He came to the point where he said to the Lord, "Anything and everything – I'm yours."

A short time later, God blessed him with the baptism in the Holy Spirit with the evidence of speaking in tongues.

He once told me, "Delores, I know that God had to break everything in me until I reached the point where I could look around my home and church and say, 'If this isn't where God wants me, I don't want to be here. If he wants me living above a store with orange crates for furniture or preaching on the street corners of this world, I'm willing.'"

The young minister did a 180-degree turn. He is totally different now. All the material things and the prominence of being the pastor of a large and influential church are gone. He now is one of the most powerful preachers I've ever heard.

The Lord spoke to him and said his daughter would be healed, saying, "Her healing is set."

He and his wife are standing on that promise.

Meanwhile, in a camp meeting in another state, God spoke to one of his friends saying that if he would stand and ask the 1,000 people there to pray for the little girl, she would be healed.

That was the confirmation.

Remember, some people are not immediately healed and I don't know why. We are never going to see a healing before God's timing is right for it could have disastrous consequences.

Inner healing sets us free and, as the Word says, when the Lord sets us free, we are free indeed (John 8:36).

Deliverance   10

Some people need deliverance especially if there is habitual sin or addiction in their lives or if they have dabbled in the occult.

While there are many causes of emotional and mental illnesses, there are times when evil spirits cause illnesses that disrupt our lives.

One of the most sinister spirits we encounter in our meetings is voodoo, a strong spirit that often comes into people through family ties.

A woman with a contorted body physically misshapen came into one of our meetings in Texas. We laid hands on her and called out the voodoo spirit. It fled and she was set free.

Usually, the voodoo spirit will try to choke a victim by causing the person's neck to swell up cutting off the breath.

Those ministering to such a victim often become fearful when they see the person beginning to choke. It is necessary for them to take authority over the evil spirit, call it out, and send it away.

On another occasion, a refined, well-educated woman came to one of our meetings. As I looked at her I had no idea what we would be dealing with later.

After the service ended, she came up to me and said she needed help.

The Lord quickened me. I knew she needed deliverance so we set a time when she would meet with me.

The Lord also impressed me that a man should accompany me to her home for the deliverance ministry. A few days later, a local pastor and I went to her beautiful home.

After the usual amenities the Lord led me to call out the fear of her father.

"Are you afraid of your father?"

"No, I'm not afraid of him."

"I'm sorry but I sense that fear and must call it out."

As we began to pray and call out that spirit, her body started shaking like a motor was running inside her. She grabbed the sides of the chair in which she was seated as her body began rising up until she was about 12 inches above the chair.

Then she started bellowing like a bull. She was so loud, her bellowing bounced off the walls and throughout the room.

I shivered and my hair stood on edge.

The pastor called out the spirit of fear and control by her father, the spirit of voodoo, and all connected spirits.

All of those evil spirits bound in the name of Jesus came out of her.

Back down in her chair she stopped bellowing and her countenance completely changed.

We rejoiced with her and departed.

That day I learned that anyone ministering deliverance must know and believe in the power of God.

Sometime later she related an incredible story to me of why she was afraid of her father. He had practiced voodoo for many years. On two occasions he had cast spells that killed two men who had stood in the way of his promotions in his profession.

She was deathly afraid of him for she feared he would also kill her if she stepped out of line.

Once delivered from voodoo spirits the woman began to grow in the Lord.

Today she leads a Bible study group.

While ministering deliverance to another woman, I heard her speaking with a man's voice.

I called out the spirit of psychic power.

"You don't want me to come out of her," a deep, guttural voice said to me. "If I come out of her, I'll come into to you for I know you well."

Frightened, I backed away as the demon spoke to me but I knew I had to cast it out.

At that point the Lord said to me, "You must cast out that demon or you'll always be afraid of them."

So, I spoke to the demon and said, "No, I'm not afraid of you and you will not come into me."

Then in the name of Jesus I called out the demon and it came out of her with a wailing moan.

"Get out of this place!" I shouted and the demon ran for his life.

There was a child that needed deliverance. I was told the child's mother was a prostitute.

God revealed to me that the child needed deliverance and healing of memories even from the womb.

I also learned he was born into the kingdom of darkness for both his mother and grandfather were involved in witchcraft and he could neither walk nor talk.

In the name of Jesus I prayed for the healing of memories for the little boy and commanded the unclean spirit that had nearly destroyed him to depart.

Later I received the report that the little boy can walk and talk and even say, "I love Jesus."

The Lord has given believers authority over demons and unclean spirits. Bill and I exercised that authority on behalf of the little boy.

The devil is so vicious he even attacks little children. Parents need to take authority over their little ones to protect them from such attacks.

One of our close friends who often visits in our home told us an incredible story of how the devil attacked his three-year-old daughter.

Our friend is a former newspaper editor and often arrived home late in the evenings.

His wife began telling him of strange things that had been happening in the house: hanging lights would begin to sway back and forth, chairs would turn around right in front of her, and other strange occurrences.

One evening she heard their three-year-old daughter scream in panic and rushed to her bedroom.

The little girl looked up at her mother with pleading eyes.

"Mommy, he said he was going to kill m.,"

"Who said that, Sweetheart?"

"He did," she answered pointing to the ceiling of the room.

That evening when the father returned home from the newspaper he and his wife prayed for their daughter's deliverance from the tormentor and in the name of Jesus cast him out of her room.

They also anointed the windows and doors of the room with oil symbolic of the protective power of the Holy Spirit.

Later that evening the little girl called her mother to her room.

"It's okay now – Jesus took care of him," she said.

There are some common demonic entryways into people's lives.

Drugs are always demonic.

A young boy came into one of our meetings so fogged he could hardly speak. He stared at us with a crazy look.

When I said hello to him it took him a long time and a great struggle just to answer me.

I touched the boy and he fell under the power and was instantly delivered from drug addiction.

Although most people don't realize it, they often open themselves up to spirits of witchcraft by fooling around with tarot cards, Ouija Boards, or by reading horoscopes in the newspapers since those horoscopes are pure astrology.

Watching movies and television shows and reading books about witchcraft and the occult can open the door to demons.

Oppression of Christians and possession of non-Christians take place so quietly, the victim doesn't notice it happening. This is what those who have been delivered from demons and addictions tell me.

A Christian also can minister deliverance to himself. Although not the easiest form of deliverance it can be done.

I never lightly consider deliverance ministry. Before getting into it I always want to know three things.

First, is there need for deliverance or for discipline? Sometimes people come to us and ask us to pray for them to be delivered from the nicotine spirit.

There is an evil spirit in nicotine but I want to make sure the evil spirit is the real root of the problem rather than the person's need for discipline and self-control.

Second, has the person done everything in his or her power to break the habit?

Third, has the person prayed to Jesus and asked for the discipline necessary to break the habit?

One of the main problems we observe among charismatic Christians is they don't seem to want to discipline themselves. They want everything to be instantaneous such as healing, inner healing, and deliverance. Remember that Jesus was the most disciplined man that ever walked the face of this earth.

Many Christians will not discipline themselves and therefore are not set free from certain bad habits. Some say demons are the source of those bad habits when in fact the source is their undisciplined old nature.

When a person honestly answers these three questions and says he or she has done everything possible to be set free, then I know a demon is at work in that person's life and deliverance is necessary. At that point I bind the demon and in the name of Jesus call it out.

There are people that no longer have control over certain areas of their lives such as rage.

Bill and I met a husband, a very gentle man, that often went into uncontrollable rages. These were totally against his character and personality. Rage would overtake him causing him to throw things around the house and even slap his loving wife.

One day he came to me and confessed his was not normal behavior and that he could always tell when the rage was welling up inside him.

He said he would fight for days to keep the rage under control then suddenly it would control him.

In the name of Jesus, I called out the demon and he was set free.

When anything controls you and makes you do things that go against your personality and beliefs, you have a demon lodged inside you and it must be cast out in order for you to be free.

Sadly, for long years many Christians didn't even realize that demons existed and therefore did not guard against them.

Many have allowed and even unwittingly invited demons into their lives but thank God we have the authority in the name of Jesus and the power of the Holy Spirit to cast them out.

Always remember, demons cannot stand for long when bound and called out in the precious name of Jesus. That is our inheritance as Christians.

Some Things to Remember   11

Because of the fall of man – the original sin – sin and sickness came into the world. Except for Jesus, it infected every person that ever lived.

Sin separates us from God but Jesus became the instrument whereby our sins could be forgiven and we could be reconciled to him.

Perhaps the Apostle Paul penned the most definitive word on the meaning of reconciliation. He wrote *"...that God was reconciling the world to Himself in Christ, not counting men's sins against them. And He committed to us the message of reconciliation"* (2 Cor. 5:19 KJV).

When we are separated from God and chained by sin, illness can come upon us but when reconciled to him our sins are forgiven and, praise God, all the blessings for which Jesus paid the price on Calvary are poured out on us and that includes healing.

Throughout the pages of this book, we have discussed various illnesses and how God often heals them. Now let's look at the roots of illness – spiritual, emotional, mental, and physical.

There are many kinds of illnesses but the most sinister are emotional or when the emotions go awry.

When dealing with those illnesses we usually have to go back through the years with the individual to find the first occurrence or root of the illness and pray for the healing of earliest memories.

Through the years I have learned I can do very little to assist the healing of memories. So, I simply walk a person through the process with Jesus. As the person allows Jesus to begin the healing, the Holy Spirit brings forth memories that have festered in the person's subconscious and of which he/she may not be consciously aware.

Neglect of the body is another cause of physical illness. The Old Testament is filled with 436 teachings on the laws that apply to good health.

The New Testament also gives us a clear teaching that addresses how a we should care for our physical bodies: *"Don't you know that you yourselves are God's temple and that God's Spirit lives in you? If anyone destroys God's temple, God will destroy him; for God's temple is sacred, and you are that temple"* (1 Cor. 3:16, 17).

Overeating that leads to overweight is among the worst of all body abuses.

As Bill and I travel throughout the land in our ministry we often encounter individuals so large they can hardly walk. Some have problems with a leg, back, stomach disorder, heart problems, and high blood pressure. It is obvious they are abusing their bodies by overeating.

Occasionally one of these dear people will say to me, "Pray for God to take this weight off of me."

We have seen God do that when he would heal an emotional or physical disorder that caused the obesity.

Ordinarily I tell the person, "I'm sorry, most of the time God doesn't deal with weight problems like that."

God wants us to be disciplined for our own good.

We have seen people with weight problems develop emotional illnesses and it is necessary to ferret out the root cause. Sometimes it is fear, doubt, anxiety, poor self-image, insecurity, and others. God often reveals the root cause and the healing begins.

Christians should get serious with God about sin in their lives for it can stand in the way of both physical and emotional healing.

The Apostle James admonishes us: *"...confess your faults one to another..."* so you can be healed (James 5:16).

If you have bad habits in your life such as smoking, drinking, and overeating, ask God to help you yield those habits to him, pray for them to be removed from your life, and God will do it.

An unforgiving spirit also can close the door to healing. When we refuse to forgive someone, we cut ourselves off from the power of God.

When you have prayed to be healed, be sure to keep a good balance as you claim the healing, a balance between the positive confession "I am healed" and "God is healing me."

I prefer the latter for it seems counterproductive to say a headache is healed when your head is splitting wide open. Or to say you are healed of arthritis when you can't open your hand or move your fingers.

The same is true when you say you are delivered from smoking when you have a cigarette between your fingers and lungs filled with tar and nicotine.

Isn't it much wiser to say "God is healing me" or "I am being healed"? That is far better since many healings are progressive.

Jesus' ministry included different methods of

healing; some instantaneous others progressive.

For instance, when Jesus was in the City of Bethsaida some people brought a blind man to him and asked him to touch him. Jesus took the blind man by the hand and led him out of the town where he applied spit to his eyes.

Then Jesus asked him if he could see.

The man looked up and said he could see men walking but they looked like trees.

Once again Jesus put his hands on the man's eyes and immediately his eyes were completely restored. (See Mark 8:22-26)

When Jesus first touched him, the blind man could have shouted the positive confession, "I'm healed! I'm healed!"

He wasn't healed but was in the process of being healed

Actually, the blind man's first response was not positive. He said, "I see men as tree, walking."

He could have run away confessing, "I'm healed!" and never been able to see men as anything but trees. However, he waited on Jesus to complete the healing and was made perfectly whole.

Be sure to confess your inability to heal yourself. That really gets God's attention and makes the devil mad.

You should say, "I can't do anything about my condition, Lord, so I am totally depending on you. You are the source of my healing; you are all I have."

We Christians can ask God to show us the source of our illness. When he reveals it to us, we can follow what he tells us to do and healing will result.

There have been times when God would not allow me to pray for someone to be healed. When my father became ill, I went to see him and wanted to pray for him to be healed. A prayer was already going through my mind something like, "Lord, just let him be with us a few more years," or "Maybe, Lord, even for a season but heal him so he can be with us a while longer."

But the minute I entered his room and walked over to his bed the Lord said, "Don't say those words."

Hence, I began to pray these words, *"Let not your heart be troubled: ye believe in God, believe also in me"* from the fourteenth chapter of the Book of John.

Then I couldn't go on for I couldn't remember the remainder of that passage of Scripture although I had taught from that passage many times.

However, as we left my father's hospital room to return home the remainder of the passage flooded through my mind.

After we arrived home my mother mentioned that I had not prayed for my father to be healed.

"You couldn't pray for him to be healed, could you." she said.

"No," I replied.

"Then he is going home and I must release him to the Lord," my mother said.

Later that evening as we prayed together, my mother said, "Lord, I don't want to give him up but I know you're calling him back to you. He has always belonged to you. But I ask that you take him quickly and free of pain."

The next day my father asked for the family lawyer so he could take care of some last-minute business even though his doctor cautioned that he might not be alert enough to speak to the lawyer.

But the next day the lawyer came and he and my father put everything in order.

My father had lived a full life and knew he was going home to be with the Lord.

He died a short time later and without pain as Mother had prayed.

After he passed away, I said, "Mom, isn't it beautiful? Now he is no longer tired, no longer sick, and Dad is seeing all the splendor of God in heaven."

That is the ultimate healing!

Walking in Victory   12

Through the years the Lord revealed to me the secret to living the victorious Christian life and the blessings of walking with him in victory.

The reader will recall that during the final stages of my terminal illness I often overcame the excruciating pain by imagining I was on a mountaintop looking down at a little river in the valley below. There in my bed I could almost smell the wildflowers and taste the clean air.

Well, guess what? Years later God took me to the exact place that during my illness had brought me much-needed relief from pain.

A minister and his wife, close friends, owned a cabin in the mountains of New Mexico. They invited me to go with them to the cabin for a few days of rest from the long days and nights of ministry.

Bill had to work but he urged me to go with them.

When we arrived at their mountain retreat, suddenly it dawned on me, "This is the exact spot God allowed me to see during my illness! The wildflowers and the little ribbon of a river down below were exactly as God had shown me earlier. Even the rock formations were the same."

What a blessing! It was a wonderful reminder of God's love for me in the darkest days of my illness.

Here's something I've learned that helps me walk in victory.

Each evening before I go to bed, I ask Jesus to show me any sins I might have committed during the day. I also ask him to take away any feelings in my heart that keep me from being obedient and free in my Christian Walk.

The Lord always answers my evening prayers and the things he reveals to me and my response are amazing.

When I first began the evening prayers and the Lord revealed certain sins to me, I argued with him by saying, "But Lord that was such a little thing."

Please remember that little sins pile up and become big sins.

Now when the Lord shows me the so-called little sins, I look at them and say, "Alright Lord, I'm laying them at the foot of the cross and asking you to forgive me right now."

If you will do this each evening before you go to sleep, you'll sleep a lot better and wake up feeling good the next morning.

When we Christians neglect prayer and reliance on God's Word, fail to fellowship with other believers, and even become careless in church attendance there will be no spiritual victories in our lives. Satan will bring illnesses back into our lives and we Christians, because of our on-again-off-again walk with the Lord, don't know how to carry on spiritual warfare in order to guard against the enemy's attacks.

Walking in victory also requires putting our lives in order and establishing the proper priorities.

We must make sure that we have accepted Jesus as our Lord and Savior. Also, we must accept the fullness of the Holy Spirit for when we receive the baptism in the Holy Spirit we experience a wonderful spiritual infilling in our lives. Without that infilling we can never receive everything God has for us.

Here's another way I'm learning to walk in victory and it is so beautiful. I carefully search the Scriptures and read all about Jesus.

"Alright, Lord, please put me right there with you and let me walk along with you during your ministry," I pray.

One day while on the phone praying for a woman from Florida concerning some spiritual problems in her life, I told her, "You must go to the Garden of Gethsemane with Jesus. You have to be right there with him as the soldiers take him away.

"You must be with him in the courtyard where he is being whipped and walk with him all the way to Calvary.

"It's important for us to be there with him when they beat him and cut his back to shreds.

"And when they pressed the crown of thorns onto his head so hard that blood flowed down over his body like a river."

As we prayed, I took her through Jesus' steps from the Garden with all the agony he endured. Then I shared with her the agony we that follow him and are crucified with Christ must endure.

"Do you see the cobblestones cut his feet?" I asked her after a pause.

In the Spirit I could see that the cobblestones had

sharp jagged points that cut his feet because the Romans had taken away his sandals leaving him barefoot.

I even saw his footprints of blood along the cobblestone road.

"That's how you learn about Jesus," I told her.

That simple exercise of walking with Jesus helped her so much that her problems seemed to fade away.

If we Christians are to live victorious lives, we must also learn to read and understand the Scriptures.

Jesus once told his detractors, *"Ye do err, not knowing the scriptures, nor the power of God"* (Matt. 22:29 KJV).

That passage of Scripture speaks so clearly to all of us today. Many know the words in their Bibles but not what they mean. How can we know unless we have the fullness of the Spirit to bring forth the truth of the Word?

We also have such misconceptions about the Holy Spirit for we know so little about him and his work.

Isn't that scary?

We must learn that he wants us to overcome the works of our Ancient Foe; wants to heal us and keep us living in abundant health; and wants to help us walk in victory.

Before his ascension into heaven Jesus gave us a wonderful promise. He said he would send "another Comforter" and when he would come, his followers would know the truth for he would teach them the truth.

What does that mean? Simply this – although Jesus is no longer here with us, the Holy Spirit took his place and that is the same as having Jesus with us.

It's Time To Be Healed

What a wonderful promise about the presence of the Holy Spirit!

Some time ago we closed out a three-week teaching seminar on healing. The last night I invited each person to trade in the ashes of their lives for the beauty of Jesus.

When we learn to do that, we will walk in victory.

From a physical standpoint walking in victory means being unwilling to accept sickness.

I probably accepted my illness because the year before I became ill my grandfather died with a deteriorated spine and cancer. I accepted the spine disease but kept telling myself that I would not die of cancer as my grandfather.

After my healing, one doctor said, "You know, Delores, we've never understood why you didn't have cancer. Your bones and every organ in your body were ripe for it."

The Lord helped me understand why I didn't get cancer – I wouldn't accept it.

I was dying in far worse condition than my grandfather but I never had cancer for I was continually rejecting it without knowing what I was doing.

We all must learn to reject the illnesses the enemy tries to put on us.

I held out my hands to him and received the spine disease, the herniated esophagus, the heart, kidney, and bowel conditions, and all the rest.

We must resist all illnesses.

If we are to walk in victory, we must guard our relationships and ask God to help us align them in proper order.

Our relationship with him is of primary importance.

We must also recognize the authority of the Scriptures to guide us on our pathway through life.

It is also necessary to nurture a good attitude. The very minute our attitudes start to turn sour we should begin praising the Lord for the good things in our lives. Savor the presence of the Holy Spirit. Rebuke the bad attitude in the name of Jesus. Take authority over it.

Now let me share with you a little secret – I hate a messy house.

Our son Chris was working on a job where he really got dirty. After he took a bath, the bathtub was always black.

Although we encouraged him to clean the bathtub, like most boys he seldom remembered. It was left for Mama to clean. Does that sound familiar?

I would look at the dirty bathtub and begin to gripe about it. Then I would get angry and think, "Why should I clean my son's dirty bathtub? He doesn't appreciate anything I do. What's the matter with Chris?"

Thankfully I learned that when something like that happened, I could start praising the Lord. I realized that instead of getting myself in an uproar, I could say, "Thank you, Jesus, that Chris is healthy. Thank you that he's not off somewhere on drugs."

You know what? When I did that, it was easy to clean that dirty black bathtub.

Satan is crafty and uses situations in the home – like a dirty bathtub – to drive a wedge between loved ones. He attacks our minds but if they are centered on Jesus, we can ward off his attacks.

When we allow a bad attitude to continue, it not only affects our families but our bodies start to feel the wear and tear of it for it affects our minds and emotions.

All Spirit-baptized believers should strive to be transparent in their lives.

Even those in ministry often are not transparent and fear sharing their doubts, fears, and mistakes.

However, the Bible never tries to hide a thing. Even the patriarchs in the Old Testament are portrayed as they really were: men with feet of clay and subject to every temptation.

Should you find that hard to believe read again the stories of Adam, Abraham – and even Sarah – Noah, David, Solomon, Simon Peter, and John Mark.

Children of God who want to walk in victory must accept the gifts of the Spirit that are available to them -- but many never do.

For instance, I'm confident there are thousands of Christians who receive the gift of the word of knowledge yet are afraid to exercise it.

During a prayer time or in a worship service God may reveal that he is healing someone. The believer who receives the word must call out the healing or Satan will try to snatch it away before the one being healed has the opportunity to receive it.

Peer pressure is also a barrier to believers acting on the word of knowledge for they don't want to be accused of being too religious.

Satan even uses peer pressure in the family.

"What will my husband think if I call out a healing?" a woman may ask,

And vice versa.

Walking in victory also means witnessing to our faith to others.

But let me issue a word of caution: We're not to try to force Jesus on anyone for that doesn't work and Jesus never did that.

There may come a time when you are having a cup of coffee with a neighbor who has a headache or some other health issue.

"You know, I believe Jesus is our healer and I would like to pray that he would take away your pain and heal you," you can say.

It's just that simple.

You can bring someone to Jesus by praying for a headache and God will heal the headache and that will be a witness to the person.

In the next day or two that person will see you and say, "Hey, you know when you prayed for me, my headache disappeared."

Thus, you have opened a door through which Jesus can walk into that person's life.

Then you open the Bible and show the person how to be saved and filled with the Holy Spirit.

It is easy to be filled with the spirit but it's quite another matter to walk in the Spirit which is much more important.

Immediately after receiving the baptism in the Holy Spirit, a believer should devour the Scriptures.

Do a word study on the Holy Spirit. Find out everything you can about his work in our lives. Then you will understand who he is, where he came from, how he worked through the Old Testament prophets, and how he came to earth to serve as the Comforter in the place of Jesus.

A Bible concordance will give you the biblical references related to him. You will also understand the nature of his ministry and the ways he works today.

After your word study on the Holy Spirit, do a word study on Jesus. You will learn all about salvation, healing, inner healing of the brokenhearted, and deliverance from unclean spirits.

You will also learn how he dealt with people such as the woman at the well (See John Chapter 4). Deep within she had a broken heart and that's why she committed adultery with so many men.

Jesus healed her and she became one of his most faithful followers.

The Holy Spirit continues the ministry of Jesus through his people. Therefore, in order to understand that work it is important for us to become intimate with Jesus.

Most Christians realize that the infilling of the Holy Spirit is not a one-time thing.

I need to be refilled for I leak.

Most of our spiritual cups also have holes in them.

We are spiritual sieves and our cups must be refilled from time to time.

One of the greatest blessings of walking in victory is we learn to experience the presence of God.

The psalmist wrote about experiencing that presence: *"You will show me the path of life; in your presence is fullness of joy; At Your right hand are pleasures forevermore"* (Psalm 16:11 NKJV).

We find so many other blessings in his presence: hope, peace, protection, comfort, provision, and others.

All these blessings are ours when we experience the presence of God and purpose in our hearts to walk in victory.

Remembrance by Bill Keith

Bill and Delores Winder were my close personal friends and they had a profound influence on my life. I remember them as quiet, humble, yet greatly anointed servants of God.

I first became acquainted with them in 1975 when Delores was ministering at a healing service at the Westminster Presbyterian Church in Shreveport, Louisiana, where the Rev. Percy Burns was the pastor.

Since I had been a member of a large denomination for many years, the Winders' ministry was new – and quite exciting – to me.

Several months later, the Rev. Dan Grove, pastor of the Mooringsport Methodist Church – where I was a member – invited Bill and Delores to our church for a healing service.

It was a memorable service. Her teaching on the work of the Holy Spirit was accompanied with signs and wonders that left an indelible impression on the members of our church.

About two years later the Winders returned to the Mooringsport church for another healing service.

After an evening service, I went to Delores and said, "Delores, you should write a book about all the miracles God has performed through your ministry."

"Bill, two years ago the Lord revealed to me that you

are the one to write my book," she said with a gentle smile.

At that time, I was a Louisiana state senator representing the people of Shreveport and a former city editor of the daily *Shreveport Journal* newspaper and already the author of several books. I considered it a great privilege to write her book.

During the next several months I spent long hours with Bill and Delores asking questions, taking notes, and learning everything about them so I could write a powerful book that would touch hundreds or even thousands of people.

It was a learning experience for me. I learned about the Holy Spirit, healing the sick, deliverance, the gifts of the Spirit, and a dozen other biblical teachings that have virtually been forgotten by the denominational churches in this land.

However, more than anything I sensed both Bill and Delores were the two most sincere people I had ever met and I grew to dearly love them.

Through the years following their ministry was like reading a new chapter in the Book of Acts. They ministered throughout this country and in several foreign lands including New Zealand, India, and Switzerland.

Delores once said that if the churches were to begin "laying on hands" for healing and casting out demons and evil spirits, there would be no need for ministries such as hers. But I don't see anything that is even close to a ministry of healing and deliverance in today's churches,

When you read of the Winders' ministry and compare it to the ministry of present-day churches

It's Time To Be Healed

in America they are as different as daylight and dark. When did you see someone healed in a church service? When did you see someone delivered from demonic oppression or possession?

Today's churches have no healing or deliverance ministries and that's unfortunate for they are filled with people with all kinds of sicknesses.

Years ago, I was invited to speak at a church in Lake Charles, Louisiana. After I greeted the congregation and thanked the pastor for inviting me, I asked, "How many of you are sick and need healing?"

Half of the congregation raised their hands including the pastor and his wife.

So, we had a healing service that night.

I'm convinced most of the churches in this land are like that Lake Charles church even though there is the clear teaching on healing in the Book of James 5:14-16 (KJV) that reads like this:

'Is any sick among you? let him call for the elders of the church; and let them pray over him, anointing him with oil in the name of the Lord:

"And the prayer of faith shall save the sick, and the Lord shall raise him up; and if he has committed sins, they shall be forgiven him."

Based on this biblical admonition, each Sunday every church in America should have a healing service. They should ask those that are sick to come to the altar where the elders of the church would anoint them with oil and pray for their healing.

But I don't see that on the horizon.

Now Bill and Delores have gone on to heaven to be with the Jesus they served so faithfully all those years after her miraculous healing in 1975 and I know it was quite a homecoming for both of them.

I'm also sure she had a wonderful reunion with Kathryn Kuhlman who was used of the Lord to set her free from the illnesses that bound her for nearly 20 years.

The tremendous spiritual influence Bill and Delores had on my life remains to this day and for that I will always be grateful.

Commentary:

The Gifts of the Spirit by Bill Keith

As you read *It's Time to be Healed* you walked with Bill and Delores Winder through their ministry of miraculous healings of the sick and infirmed and deliverance for those bound and chained by evil spirits.

You also received a clear teaching on the work of the Holy Spirit and the gifts of the Spirit in today's world.

However, I recognize you may not fully understand and may have reservations about the miracles described herein, miracles so evident in Delores' ministry.

During my interviews with Bill and Delores I heard the term percutaneous cordotomy for the first time and I was quite curious about this amazing medical procedure. Although I did not question how the Winders explained it to me, I decided to learn more about it.

I contacted a prominent neurosurgeon in Shreveport and asked for an interview which he granted.

After thanking him for seeing me, I asked him to explain the percutaneous cordotomy procedure to me.

He confirmed everything Delores' doctors explained to her about the procedure.

I was particularly interested in the result of the procedure that once the nerve centers are burned out, they can never be reversed.

He said that medical science has no way to reverse the procedure.

I felt the information from the neurosurgeon confirmed everything Delores and Bill told me about Delores' amazing medical journey.

The reason some people find it difficult to understand the gifts of the Spirit – such as the gift of healing -- is because they do not see those gifts operating today in the vast majority of our churches.

Hence, Delores' ministry was totally different from the ministry in nearly all of our churches.

Jesus had a twofold ministry – teaching and preaching and healing and deliverance.

However, today's ministers – with a few exceptions – follow only half of his ministry and that is preaching and teaching.

I believe the reason most ministers limit their ministries only to teachings and preaching can be found in the Protestant Reformation in the 16th Century and the teachings of great Christian theologians Martin Luther, John Calvin, Huldrych Zwingli, and others.

These three great scholars were cessationists who believed the gifts of the Spirit described in the New Testament and Book of Acts ceased after the 1st Century of Christianity and therefore should not be included in church doctrine today.

They taught that miracles such as healing and deliverance were given only to provide support and validate the ministry of Jesus and later that of the apostles.

Why did they disbelieve in the miraculous? I think they believed the day of miracles had passed because in their day they never witnessed any of those miracles in their churches.

Also, they relied on two passages of Scripture found in I Corinthians chapter 13.

Verse eight in the King James Version reads like this: "Love never fails. But whether there are prophecies, they will fail; whether there are tongues, they will cease; whether there is knowledge, it will vanish away."

Those who believe the gifts of the Spirit have ended use this verse to support their position on the matter. Verse 8 does say "prophesies will fail" and tongues will cease."

But it also says "knowledge, it will vanish."

I raise the question: has knowledge vanished along with prophecies and tongues? I don't think so.

Our detractors like to quote another section of the verse about prophecies and tongues passing away, but they do not add the word knowledge.

The great reformers believed this verse applied to the post-apostolic period.

However, let me make this quite clear, there is not one verse of Scripture that even hints that the gifts of the Spirit went away after the time of Jesus and the apostles and are not for today

Several major denominations embrace all or part of so-called Reform Theology. They include Presbyterian, Congregational, Reformed, Anglican (Episcopal), and some Baptists.

The majority of today's Christians look askance at the ministry of healing and deliverance but their strongest opposition is toward the slain in the Spirit religious phenomenon. They believe these experiences

– as often described in Delores' book – are far beyond the pale.

Since I have a great deal of first-hand experience on this subject, I want to share my insight on being slain in the Spirit with you the reader.

There are several terms used for this spiritual experience. Delores always referred to it as "slain in the Spirit." Others refer to it as "resting in the Spirit" or "falling out under the power."

Whatever the description, there are several Scriptures that refer to it.

11 Chronicles 5:14 tells us that the priests could not stand to minister because the glory of the Lord filled the house of worship.

Remember when Judas brought the soldiers to arrest Jesus?

"Who do you seek?" he asked them,

"Jesus of Nazareth," they answered.

When Jesus said "I am he," the soldiers backed away and fell to the ground." We find this true story in John chapter 18.

When the Apostle John exiled on the Isle of Patmos saw the glorified Jesus he fell to his feet as a dead man, according to Revelation 1:17.

Let me now share some historical information of this spiritual phenomenon in our country.

During the First Great Awakening (1730s and 1740s) revival spread like wildfire throughout the American colonies.

The ministries of Jonathan Edwards and George Whitefield reported numbers of believers slain in the Spirit during their meetings.

Both Edwards and Whitefield and other evangelicals believed the experience of being slain in the Spirit was not a new phenomenon to the evangelical movement.

John Wesley ((1703-1791) the founder of the Methodist Church, referred to the slain in the Spirit phenomenon as the "....outward sign that so often accompanied the inward work of God."

Wesley reported that during one of his meetings, the entire congregation fell to the floor as though dead.

Perhaps the most prevalent occurrences of being slain in the Spirit occurred during the Kane Ridge Revival (Aug. 6-13, 1801) in Kane Ridge, Kentucky It was the largest of all camp meetings during the Second Great Awakening (1790-1840).

Although the revival lasted only eight days, those eight days changed America. The people sang, shouted, clapped their hands, and hugged and kissed one another. Others prayed all night singing and praising God.

An estimated 3,000 of those attending the meeting were slain in the Spirit.

That eight-day revival changed America as those who were there carried the revival message all across the land.

The slain in the Spirit was prevalent during the great Charismatic Revival of the 1960 and 70s as the revival touched millions of the people of our land from most every denomination.

I also want to tell you about my personal experience.

Back in 1973 I attended a Full Gospel Businessmen's meeting in New Boston, Texas, where Odell McBrayer, a prominent Fort Worth attorney, was the featured speaker.

After his message, he invited those who wanted prayer to come to the altar. As he prayed for them, several were slain in the Spirit.

I wanted to ask the speaker a question but did not want to fall and join several others on the floor. So, I decided that if I held on tightly to his shoulders there would be no way I could fall.

I made my way to the altar, reached out and held his shoulders. But as soon as I began to ask my question, I fell to the floor.

I was out for some time and when I awakened, I could barely stand and another family member had to drive me home.

Amazingly, I felt like I was drunk for the next two days.

I will never understand how it all happened but it was a wonderful spiritual experience.

God ministered the baptism of the Holy Spirit to me as I rested in him and endowed me with two gifts of the Spirit – healing and the word of knowledge.

After that, I had a wonderful healing ministry.

I prayed for a blind man and God opened his eyes, a deaf man and God opened his ears, another man with a severed spine, and still another with seven blood clots were healed.

I prayed for a woman with pneumonia and she returned home that day.

My wife Vivian Marie and I prayed for her nephew who was dying of a liver disease. The doctors said if he didn't receive a liver transplant he would live only a few days.

Vivian and I anointed him with oil in obedience to James 5:14.

Two days later he returned home.

My wife also received the baptism in the Holy Spirit and for long years has prayed for the sick and infirmed and seen numerous miracles.

She prayed for another man with a terminal liver disease. When he went to see his doctor, he could find no trace of the liver disease.

One of Vivian's friends was facing serious heart surgery because her arteries were virtually closed. But before the surgery she called my wife and asked for prayer. When she went to the hospital the doctors decided to X-ray her heart one more time.

They found no evidence of any heart disease!

I pray that the information in this commentary on the Gifts of the Spirit will bless and encourage you to receive and exercise the wonderful gifts of the Spirit.

About the Author

Bill Keith served as a Southern Baptist missionary in Japan for seven years, was a war correspondent in Vietnam on a mission for the White House, and had other assignments in Tokyo, the Philippines, and West Berlin.

Back in the states, he became a reporter, city editor, and editor of three newspapers in Louisiana and Texas.

He graduated from Wheaton College in Wheaton, Illinois, with a Bachelor of Arts degree in writing and the Southwestern Baptist Theological Seminary in Fort Worth, Texas, with a Master of Divinity degree. He also received a certificate of graduation from the Naganuma School of the Japanese Language in Tokyo after five years of study.

While with the *Shreveport Times* newspaper he won numerous awards for investigative reporting. Later with the *Shreveport Journal,* he was a so-called "stringer" for *Time Magazine.*

He wrote an op-ed piece for *USA TODAY*, was an instructor in journalism at Louisiana State University-Shreveport, and served in the Louisiana Senate representing the people of Northwest Louisiana.

In 2010, Keith – who has written 26 books -- granted permission to the Military Chaplains Association to reprint 5,000 copies of his book *Days of Anguish, Days of Hope* (the story of a heroic military chaplain during World War II). They gave copies of the book to all active military chaplains and to the 535 members of Congress.

The chaplains honored him with an Honorary Life Membership in their Association.

Together he and his wife Vivian Marie live in West Texas. They have six children and twelve grandchildren.

Made in the USA
Coppell, TX
01 March 2026

72676136R00100